W9-BYR-184

BUILDING
Shelves
IN A WEEKEND

BUILDING
Shelves
IN A WEEKEND

15 step-by-step woodworking projects

ALAN AND GILL BRIDGEWATER

POPULAR WOODWORKING BOOKS
Cincinnati, Ohio

First published in North America
in 2000 by Popular Woodworking Books
an imprint of F&W Publications, Inc.
1507 Dana Avenue
Cincinnati, OH 45207
1-800/289-0963

10 9 8 7 6 5 4 3 2 1

ISBN 1-55870-548-1

Managing Editor: Coral Walker

Designed and created for New Holland by AG&G BOOKS
Design: Glyn Bridgewater
Illustrators: Alan and Gill Bridgewater
Shelf design: Alan Bridgewater
Photography: Ian Parsons
Editor: Kay McMullan
Woodwork: Barry Biddlecombe
Wood species: The Art Veneers Co Ltd

Reproduction by Modern Age Repro House Ltd, Hong Kong
Printed and bound in Malaysia by Times Offset (M) sdn Bhd

The information in this book is true and complete to the best of our knowledge. All
recommendations are made without guarantee on the part of the authors and the publishers.
The authors and publishers disclaim any liability for damages or injury resulting from the use of
this information.

CONVERSION CHART

To convert the imperial measurements given in this book to metric measurements,
simply multiply the figure given in the text by the relevant number shown in the table
below. Bear in mind that conversions will not necessarily work out exactly, and you
will need to round the figure up or down slightly. (Do not use a combination of
imperial and metric measurements — for accuracy, keep to one system.)

To convert	Multiply by
inches to millimeters	25.4
feet to meters	0.3048
yards to meters	0.9144
sq inches to sq millimeters	64.516
sq feet to sq meters	0.0929
sq yards to sq meters	0.8361
cu feet to cu meters	0.0283
cu yards to cu meters	0.7645
pounds to grams	453.59
pounds to kilograms	0.4535
gallons to liters	3.785

CONTENTS

INTRODUCTION

Shelves are everywhere about us: shelves for dishes in the kitchen, office shelves for files, shelves for book collections, shelves in our bedrooms, dens, workshops and sun rooms. Just about everything we eat, drink, wear, read, or consult spends a good part of its time sitting on a shelf. And the funny thing is, no matter how many shelves we have around home and hearth, there is always a need for more.

Characteristically, a shelf or shelving unit is made up of one or more horizontal members – boards or battens – that are fixed within a structure or frame, the simplest shelf being no more than a wooden board bridged across a couple of store-bought brackets. Shelves are the very foundation of the American and European furniture-making tradition. No sooner did farmers and settlers build a shed, shack, or shanty, than they started to build shelves. One could argue that they had no choice but to build functional shelves – how else could they keep their goods dry and off the ground? But then again, if the task of building shelves was simply one of function and practical needs, why did these home-building woodworkers go out of their way to create such a dynamic array of forms?

From the woodworker's point of view, there is something really exciting and challenging about making a good strong shelf; it's almost as if the ability to make a display rack, or an oak bookcase, is a gauge against which the woodworker's ability and expertise are judged.

In this book, we have designed the projects so that they can easily be made by all woodworkers, from the inexperienced beginner with a basic tool kit who needs to build a low-cost functional shelf, to the more accomplished woodworker who wants to make a prestigious design statement. As to the skill level – you don't have to be a woodworking genius, you just have to be enthusiastic and enjoy a good challenge.

We show you in painstaking, hands-on-tool detail how to make fifteen different classic and traditional forms – from a color-washed kitchen shelf that is refreshingly joyous in its naïve simplicity, to a magnificent, formal, oak bookshelf, and a wide range of exciting, challenging, and intriguing shelves in between.

Each project opens with an introduction to put the piece in context: its background, inspiration, and design considerations; then we show you how to make it. With extensive tool and cutting lists, traditional working drawings, design variations, pen-and-wash illustrations, trouble-shooting answers, and step-by-step photographs, we tell you just about everything you need to know about the project. Then again, if you want to know more about a particular tool or a certain joint, the **Tools, Materials,** and **Techniques** section on page 8 will show you the way.

Don't worry if you are a nervous beginner: we have included a good number of projects to get you launched. Just close your eyes and imagine. No more precious books piled in heaps on the floor, sad and sagging hand-me-down shelves, or treasures

rolling around and gathering dust. You can now organize your life and enrich your home with an exciting and eye-stopping array of classic and traditional shelves.

Build a good, sound, oak shelf for your tools, and a fine and fancy shelf for your books, and the rest is easy. Best of luck!

Alan & Gill

HEALTH AND SAFETY

Woodworking procedures are potentially dangerous. Before starting work, check through the following list:

- Make sure you are not going to get dragged into machines. Tie back hair, roll up sleeves, and remove jewelry.
- Follow the manufacturer's instructions when making adjustments to machines.
- Make sure guards are in place. Never operate a machine if you are tired or under medication.

- Make sure all electrics conform to recommended standards.
- Wear a dust-mask and goggles.
- When using MDF, wear a mask and use a dust extractor.
- When using chisels, always cut away from your body.
- Have a first-aid kit and telephone within easy reach.

About this book

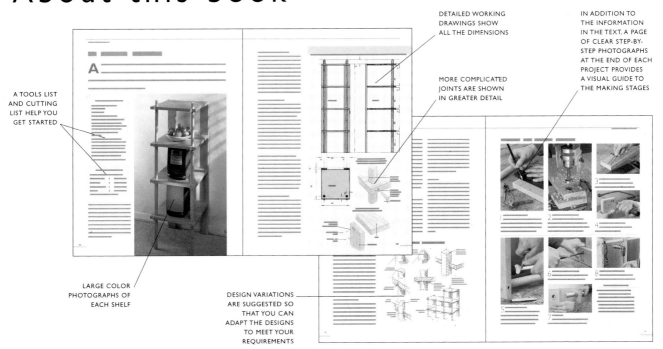

DETAILED WORKING DRAWINGS SHOW ALL THE DIMENSIONS

IN ADDITION TO THE INFORMATION IN THE TEXT, A PAGE OF CLEAR STEP-BY-STEP PHOTOGRAPHS AT THE END OF EACH PROJECT PROVIDES A VISUAL GUIDE TO THE MAKING STAGES

A TOOLS LIST AND CUTTING LIST HELP YOU GET STARTED

MORE COMPLICATED JOINTS ARE SHOWN IN GREATER DETAIL

LARGE COLOR PHOTOGRAPHS OF EACH SHELF

DESIGN VARIATIONS ARE SUGGESTED SO THAT YOU CAN ADAPT THE DESIGNS TO MEET YOUR REQUIREMENTS

PART ONE

Tools, techniques, and materials

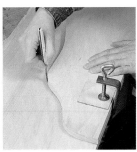

While undoubtedly there is very special pleasure to be had from working with wood, you also need to have a clear understanding of your tools and materials, and be fully conversant with woodworking techniques. The unique pleasure of woodworking stems from the fact that the different characteristics of individual woods require you to be flexible and adventurous in your approach. For the best results, be aware of the grain, texture, and workability of different types of wood, and find out about tools and how to choose the best ones for the job.

POWER TOOLS AND TRADITIONAL HAND TOOLS

Though traditionally most woodworkers used hand tools, there is now an increasing push towards using power tools. For making the shelves in this book, we recommend using the machines and tools illustrated below. If you only have hand tools, you can buy wood cut and planed to size.

POWER PLANING TOOLS

Machine planing involves surfacing the lumber to square up the face side and face edge, and thicknessing it to plane the remaining surfaces true to the face side and face edge. Home wood-workers generally opt for using a dual-purpose planer-thicknesser.

A modern planer-thicknesser – ideal for a small workshop – set up for surfacing.

WOODTURNING TOOLS

Use a lathe for making dowels, spindles, pegs, and knobs. The workpiece is rotated at speed, while at the same time a hand-held scraper or gouge is advanced until it comes into contact and cuts the wood.

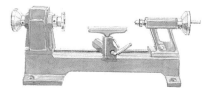

A bench-top lathe – a choice machine for home woodworkers.

POWER SAWS

There are four basic machine-sawing options: a table saw for cutting timber to size, a radial-arm saw for cutting wood to length, a band saw for cutting broad curves in thick stock, and a scroll saw for cutting tight curves in thin wood. Most woodworkers opt for a mix of power and hand saws.

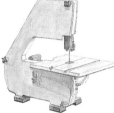
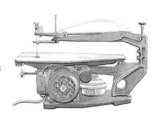

Radial-arm saw – a versatile machine – for crosscutting, ripping, and grooving.

Band saw – for making curved cuts in thick-section wood.

Scroll saw – for cutting small, tight, complex curves in thin wood.

MEASURING AND MARKING TOOLS

All woodwork starts with measure-ments and marks. You need: a rule and a metal straightedge for laying out, a try square for drawing right angles, a single-pin gauge for running lines, a mortise gauge for setting out joints, a trammel for drawing large circles, callipers for measuring turned diame-ters, a single-bevel knife and scratch awl for scoring the line of cut, and a collection of pencils.

A mortise gauge for scoring parallel lines when marking out mortise joints.

A tape measure – ideal for preliminary laying out.

A combined marking knife (left end) and scratch awl (right end).

A try square – with a wooden stock and a steel blade.

HAND SAWS

Hand sawing is central to good wood-working. You need a crosscut saw for cutting across the grain, a rip saw for cutting in the direction of the grain, a backsaw and a gents saw for cutting joints, and a coping or bow saw for cutting curves.

A crosscut saw is designed for cutting stock across the run of the grain.

A backsaw (tenon saw) is ideal for cutting joints by hand.

CHISELS

Chisels are crucial to woodworking. The best advice is to start out with a set of four top-quality bevel-edged cabinetmaker's chisels ranging in size from $\frac{1}{4}$ in, $\frac{3}{8}$ in, $\frac{5}{8}$ in, to $\frac{7}{8}$ in – and then get other types as the need arises.

The bevel-edge chisel is designed for general paring and joint finishing.

The socketed mortise chisel is used with a mallet for chopping mortise holes.

The heavy, traditional mortise chisel – with its massive handle – is used in conjunction with a heavy mallet.

THE ROUTER

If you enjoy working with machines then a hand-held router is a great option for variously cutting grooves, rabbets, moldings, and joints. A vast range of cutters is available. You will need to kit yourself out with a dust-mask and ear defenders.

A router, used with specific cutters, is an efficient tool for making swift joints and profiles.

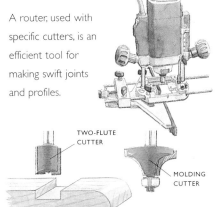

TWO-FLUTE CUTTER

MOLDING CUTTER

CLAMPS

Clamps are used throughout wood-working. C-clamps, hold-downs, hold-fasts, bar clamps, hand-screws, pipe clamps, quick clamps, and spring clamps are all devices used to hold wood secure. You can never have enough clamps – the more you have, the greater your control options. Always go for best-quality "forged" clamps – because cheap cast clamps are likely to fail.

HAND PLANES

Most woodworkers use three planes: a bench plane, a block plane, and a rabbet plane. You might also use a bull-nose plane for cleaning up joints, a hollow plane for edge profiles, and a grooving plane for jointing.

The bench plane – used for levelling and smoothing long grain.

DRILLING

Woodworkers need to bore holes. Ideally, you need a drill press, a brace, a hand drill, and a good selection of auger, twist, flat, and forstner bits.

An auger bit is used in conjunction with a brace for boring deep, straight holes.

Twist bits are mainly used in power drills for boring small-diameter holes.

A forstner bit being used in a drill press – the best set-up for boring accurate, large-diameter holes.

A bar or sash clamp for clamping planked surfaces and jointed frames.

A C-clamp – used when there is a need for strength.

A quick-release clamp for light clamping jobs.

The block plane for trimming end grain.

The wooden rabbet plane – with its adjustable toe – is well suited to cutting long rabbets.

MATERIALS AND WOOD TYPES

While a good part of the pleasure of woodworking has to do with the fact that no two pieces of wood are identical, you do need to minimize the risk of using an inappropriate piece of wood by being aware of the characteristics of various materials.

MANUFACTURED BOARDS

Though there is a wide range of manufactured boards currently available, most woodworkers opt for using best veneer-core plywood, and/or medium density fibreboard (MDF), in conjunction with high-quality veneers.

Multi-veneer plywood is very strong and stable.

MDF works to a crisp-edged finish.

Chipboard is suitable for interior veneer work.

PRE-MILLED LUMBER

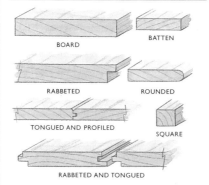

BOARD   BATTEN

RABBETED   ROUNDED

TONGUED AND PROFILED

SQUARE

RABBETED AND TONGUED

A selection of readily available planed and profiled sections for general construction.

Wood is variously sold as S2S (surfaced two sides), S3S (surfaced two sides and ripped one edge), and S4S (surfaced all sides). Don't count on milled wood being square and true.

FAULTS IN LUMBER

To a greater or lesser extent, lumber is always faulted. Avoid the major faults below by closely inspecting your wood at the time of purchase.

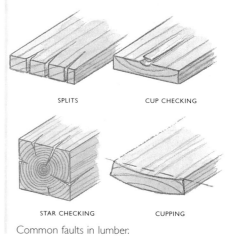

SPLITS   CUP CHECKING

STAR CHECKING   CUPPING

Common faults in lumber.

ALLOWING FOR MOVEMENT IN WOOD

A solid slab of wood will always, to a greater or lesser extent, shrink and expand to accommodate changing atmospheric conditions – with the movement always being greater across the width than along the length. A good part of the designing and building procedure is to figure out how to avoid and/or disguise the effects of any movement. Slotted screw hardware, frame and loose-panel construction, sliding joints, and tongue-and-groove jointed boards are all methods of coping with the inevitable movement.

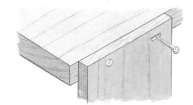

Screw and slot joints allow for dimensional movement across the grain.

A loose-wedged tenon allows the joint to be tightened when the wood shrinks.

The stopped dado ensures that movement within the joint is hidden.

Tongue-and-groove construction disguises the inevitable movement.

TYPES OF WOOD

There are thousands of species of tree – all varying greatly in size, color, and character. Some trees yield wide, beautifully figured boards that are a pleasure to work – hardly any knots, no splits, and a firm, clean texture – while others yield narrow, character-less boards that are variously crumbly to the touch, or so hard that they blunt the tools. The secret of good woodwork is being able to confidently select a piece of wood that is appropriate to your needs. We have chosen to use a relatively small range of non-endangered native American and European wood – species that have traditionally been used for building furniture and interiors.

You can buy this lumber rough-sawn, or planed smooth in useful standard thicknesses.

American maple: A creamy-colored, close-grained, smooth-textured, difficult-to-work hardwood – cuts clean with a fair finish. Readily available in good, knot-free widths and lengths.

European pine: A creamy to pinkish yellow-brown, straight-grained, coarse-textured, knotty softwood. A good choice for experimental forms, and for bold designs.

American cherry: A straight-grained, fine-textured, creamy pink-to-brown hardwood. Works to a smooth, high-shine finish – perfect for hand-tool work.

English cherry: A cream to pink-brown, strong-textured hardwood – works to a dynamic, high-shine finish. Coarser and available in shorter widths and lengths than its American cousin.

European birch: A pale cream to yellow-brown, straight-grained, strong and stable, easy-to-work hardwood – readily available in generous widths and lengths.

Cedar: Known as "true" cedar, Mount Lebanon cedar, and many other names besides. A brown, straight-grained softwood. Traditionally used for top-quality interior joinery and furniture.

English larch: A pinky, brown-white, straight-grained, resinous, even-textured softwood – available in good widths and lengths. Difficult to work, but compensates by being very flexible and strong along its length.

English beech: A straight-grained, even-textured, brownish-white hardwood – readily available in good widths and lengths. Excellent for planing and jointing, and really good for shelves. It works to a hard and smooth finish.

Douglas fir: A reddish-brown, straight, coarse-grained softwood – available in good widths and lengths. Exciting grain pattern with good resistance to bowing. Works to a hard, smooth, high-shine finish.

American red oak: A pink-brown, biscuit-colored, coarse, straight-grained hardwood. Available in good, knot-free widths and lengths – good for shelves. Relatively easy to work – finishes well.

JOINTS AND HARDWARE

While jointing is primarily a procedure that has to do with function – how to join a number of elements to make a satisfactory whole – the ability to cut a joint that is both functional and decorative is considered by most to be a measure of a woodworker's skill. The projects show the joints in detail.

TYPES OF JOINTS *All the joints below are glued and clamped once made*

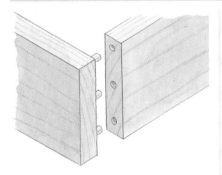

Dowel joint
The dowel joint is a butt joint re-inforced with pegs that are pushed into carefully aligned holes that are drilled into the parts being joined. The dowel joint is a swift substitute for dado, tenon, and dovetail joints.

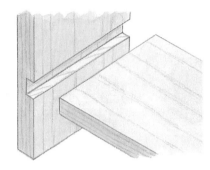

Through dado joint
The through dado, through groove, or through housing joint is much favored by shelf builders. The easy-to-make design allows for movement across the width of the grain. The joint is both strong and stable.

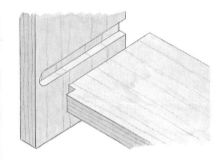

Stopped dado joint
The stopped dado joint is an exten-sion of the through dado – with the same mechanical characteristics. The stopped end of the groove and the notched end of the shelf results in the end of the dado being hidden.

Slot mortise joint
Known also as an open mortise and a bridle joint, the slot mortise joint is a variation on the tenon. This joint is sometimes reinforced by inserting a peg or a third component through the assembled joint.

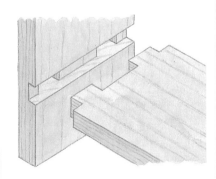

Stub tenon joint
The stub tenon joint, also known as housed pins, and housing tenons, provides a strong joint for shelves. Depending upon usage, the tenons can be stopped so that they are hidden, or cut through and wedged.

Dovetail joint
The open or through dovetail is a choice joint for shelf-making. The design of the joint is such that pulling or forces on the joint – piles of books on the bottom shelf – results in the joint locking tight.

GLUING JOINTS

A good glue bond, with just the right amount of the correct type of glue, is essential to the strength of most joints. Before gluing, have a trial dry run to choose the clamps, arrange the clamping area, and generally to consider the order of work.

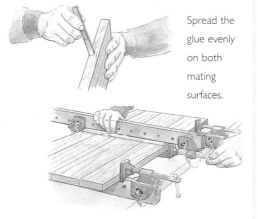

Spread the glue evenly on both mating surfaces.

Place a piece of paper between the clamp and the workpiece, and tighten up until a bead of glue oozes out.

USING SCREWS

While we wouldn't recommend the use of screws for top-quality work – much better to have a joint – they are an option when there is the need for the shelves to be swiftly dismantled. No matter what the choice of screws – brass, steel, or whatever – the secret of success is to use a screw of the correct length, and to drill a pilot hole.

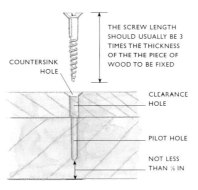

COUNTERSINK HOLE

THE SCREW LENGTH SHOULD USUALLY BE 3 TIMES THE THICKNESS OF THE THE PIECE OF WOOD TO BE FIXED

CLEARANCE HOLE

PILOT HOLE

NOT LESS THAN ⅛ IN

Choose a screw with a length three times the thickness of the piece being fixed.

KNOCK-DOWN HARDWARE

Knock-down hardware is a good idea when you want to build a piece that can be swiftly disassembled. Commonly, such hardware is designed for square-cut, butt-joint construction. All you do is bore a number of carefully positioned holes, slide the hardware in place, and tighten up with a screwdriver or wrench.

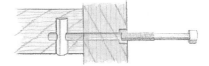

A bolt and toggle fixing is an easy-to-fix solution for joining two members.

Plastic screw-blocks are a swift option for fixing utilitarian shelves.

FIXING SHELVES TO WALLS

Shelf-makers are commonly presented with two tricky problems: how to fit shelves directly to the wall, and how to fit shelves in an existing bay, alcove, or niche. Our solutions cater for fixing shelves to either solid (brick and plaster), or hollow (stud and board) walls. The illustrations show a selection of brackets and wall hardware.

Handmade brackets

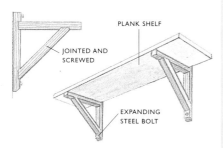

PLANK SHELF

JOINTED AND SCREWED

EXPANDING STEEL BOLT

A traditional braced or gallows bracket plugged and bolted to a solid wall.

Store-bought brackets

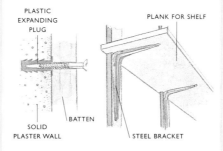

PLASTIC EXPANDING PLUG

PLANK FOR SHELF

SOLID PLASTER WALL

BATTEN

STEEL BRACKET

Plug and screw battens to the solid wall, and then screw steel brackets to the battens.

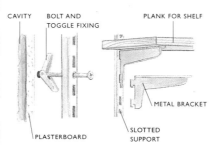

CAVITY

BOLT AND TOGGLE FIXING

PLANK FOR SHELF

PLASTERBOARD

METAL BRACKET

SLOTTED SUPPORT

The supports are fixed to the hollow wall and then the brackets are slotted into place.

Alcove shelving for solid walls

Battens are screwed to the sides of the alcove and bridged by a thick plank shelf.

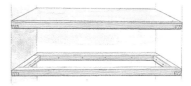

A frame is screwed to the walls and topped off with plywood or similar.

Side planks are drilled to take shelf support studs – for shelf height adjustment.

FINISHING MATERIALS AND TECHNIQUES

If you are going to the trouble of building a top-quality shelf, you need to work diligently through all the stages – planing, sanding, scraping, and rubbing down – before choosing a finish to enhance the wood and to create a surface that is easy to maintain, a pleasure to touch, and a delight to the eye.

PLANING END GRAIN

After you have assembled a project it is sometimes necessary to rework, smooth, and level end grain. Using a plane and a supporting block of waste wood allows the plane to run through without splitting the grain.

Clamp the waste wood to the side of the workpiece – so that it receives the brunt as the plane runs through.

SANDING

Preparing the surface is essential for a good finish. Sanding is the technique of using graded abrasive paper to cut back the fibers of the wood. Abrasive papers are sold according to grit size – the smaller the grit, the finer the cut.

The traditional folding and tearing of the sandpaper results in the grit surfaces never meeting face to face.

SANDPAPER FITS OVER FOAM PAD

An orbital power sander leaves a finish that minimizes hand sanding.

Use a sanding block and aluminum oxide paper to rub down flat surfaces to a fine finish. Work with the grain.

SCRAPING

Scraper planes allow you to finish large, broad surfaces without the need for sanding. Cabinet scrapers are used for smoothing all types of surface – flat, convex, and concave.

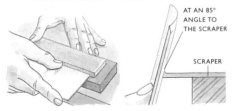

AT AN 85° ANGLE TO THE SCRAPER

SCRAPER

Use a medium stone to hone the cabinet scraper blade to a clean, square-cut edge. Hold the scraper flat down on the bench and run a burnisher at an angle to create a burr.

The scraper plane is held with two hands and run at a shearing angle to the direction of the grain.

Using a cabinet scraper blade for smoothing out selected areas of rough, torn grain.

RUBBING DOWN

De-nibbing: ultra-fine sanding to cut back the wood fibers that are left standing proud after sealing the wood.

Rubbing down is the complete process of using scrapers and abrasives to cut back the fibers of the wood in order to achieve a smooth finish. The greater the time spent rubbing down and the finer the abrasives, the smoother the finish.

DANISH OIL AND WAX FINISH

Oil and beeswax give a wonderfully swift and easy finish. You don't have to worry about runs, dribbles, and brush marks, there are no worries about toxic vapours, the finish doesn't crack or flake, and, best of all, pure beeswax is a natural product. While the finish is beautiful to look at, it is not hard-wearing. It is most important that you specify pure beeswax when purchasing.

2 Wipe the surface over with an oil-soaked cloth and let it dry.

1 Prepare the ground by vacuuming up the dust and wiping the surface over with a clean, cotton cloth. Have a final check for excess glue around joints.

3 Swab the surface over with a small amount of beeswax and then use a lint-free cotton cloth to burnish the surface to a sheen.

VARNISH FINISH

Varnish is a hard-wearing, waterproof finish that dries to give a matt, sheen, or high-gloss effect. While specific varnishes might be clear or tinted, and oil- or water-based, they are all characterized by the fact that they sit on the surface rather than soak in.

1 Dilute a small quantity of varnish with mineral spirits, and paint on in the direction of the grain.

2 Rub down with fine-grade sandpaper, wipe away the dust, and brush on the final coat.

ALTERNATIVE FINISHING EFFECTS

Wire brushing

Wire brushing is a swift way of achieving a surface that reveals the grain. The finish fools the eye into believing the wood has been weathered like driftwood or desert wood.

1 Use a power tool fitted with a rotary steel brush to remove the soft grain.

2 Use a hand brush to exaggerate the "weathering" on selected corners.

Liming

Liming is the procedure of filling the grain with a white paste and then rubbing back, so as to create a worn and sun-bleached effect – as if the wood has been whitewashed.

1 Sand the wood and then use a cloth to work the liming paste into the pores of the grain.

2 Wipe across the grain with a coarse cloth and then burnish with beeswax.

Distressing

Distressing is an effect that is used to imitate the wear and tear seen on pieces of old furniture. This variously involves sanding back paint, bruising, and softening edges.

1 Paint with two contrasting colours, and dent the wood with a hammer and wire.

2 Cut through the paint with steel wool and finish with a thin wash of burnt ocher.

PART TWO

Projects

One of the joys of making traditional and classic shelves is that you can, to a great extent, change the specifications, imagery, materials, jointing procedures, tools used, and techniques to suit your own needs and fancies. You might want a shelf bigger or smaller, made from a different wood, designed with larger curves, worked with different tools, constructed with different joints, or whatever. The best way forward is to have a good, long look at the various working drawings, photographs, and design variations, consider the costings, and then, in the light of your tool kit, skill level, and requirements, to go your own way.

1: COLUMN BOOKCASE

This oak bookcase was inspired by the notion that there are fledgling woodworkers out there who, while they are very keen to build a good-size, designer bookcase, are limited by a minimal tool kit – say a couple of saws, a couple of planes, a drill press, and not much else – and lack of experience.

TOOLS AND MATERIALS

- rip saw or pre-milled lumber
- crosscut saw
- marking gauge
- bench plane
- bar clamp slightly longer than the board width
- drill press (or brace)
- forstner drill bit, 1 in diameter
- square, dividers, rule, and pencil
- mallet
- power sander and graded sandpaper
- PVA glue
- Danish oil and beeswax polish
- American oak and cherry (see cutting list)

CUTTING LIST		
part	quantity	L x W x T
oak side boards	2	707 x 13 x 1½
oak shelves	6	11 x 13 x 1½
cherry dowels	24	3 x 1 diam.
(finished sizes, given in inches)		

If you have ambitions to build something prestigious – a real design statement – but don't enjoy cutting dovetails, tenons, and the like, then this is a choice project. It's big, it's bold, and it's totally free from difficult-to-cut traditional joints. All that is required is that you can saw a straight line, plane accurately, and drill a series of well-placed holes. The dowels are both functional and decorative.

Considering the design

Look at the working drawings and notes. See how this bookcase uses the same thickness and width of wood throughout. The shelves are butt jointed and fixed with giant-size dowels, and the pattern of the dowels becomes a design feature.

There are only a few procedures — but the success of the project hinges on working with a fair degree of accuracy, keeping the ends of the shelves absolutely square and flush, and making sure the holes are run dead center into the thickness of the wood. Note we use American oak for the unit, and cherry or another dark wood for the dowels.

Preparing and laying out the wood

Having carefully selected your wood — the two long side boards, and the one or more pieces that go to make the six shelves, set them down in the workshop and check them over to make sure that they are free from potential problems. If there are small knots or twists in the grain — and this is likely with some species of oak — then make sure that they are placed either on the inside face of the long boards, and/or on the underside of the shelves.

When you have selected your wood, square it to length and cut it to size with the crosscut saw. Cut the two long boards to 1 in oversize at 71 in, and the wood that goes to make the six shelf boards into one or two manageable lengths.

Facing the boards with the bench plane

Take your sawn boards, check them by hand and eye to identify the high spots, and then mark the high spots with a soft pencil. Clamp the board down flat on the bench and run skimming cuts across the width to cut off the high spots as marked. Tilt the plane on its side and use the edge of the plane's sole to sight down the board, and once again mark any high spots. Continue sighting, marking, and planing until the surface is level. When you have planed one face, set the marking gauge to 1½ in, and score a guide line around the edges and ends. Rerun the planing on the other face until you reach the gauged line.

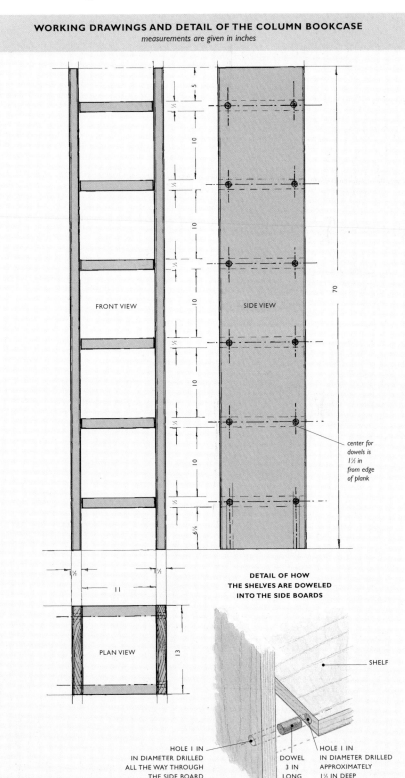

WORKING DRAWINGS AND DETAIL OF THE COLUMN BOOKCASE
measurements are given in inches

FRONT VIEW

SIDE VIEW

center for dowels is 1½ in from edge of plank

PLAN VIEW

DETAIL OF HOW THE SHELVES ARE DOWELED INTO THE SIDE BOARDS

SHELF

HOLE 1 IN
IN DIAMETER DRILLED
ALL THE WAY THROUGH
THE SIDE BOARD

DOWEL
3 IN
LONG

HOLE 1 IN
IN DIAMETER DRILLED
APPROXIMATELY
1½ IN DEEP

Planing the edges

Sight down the edge and mark in the high spots with a soft pencil. Let's say that you have identified three high spots. Secure the board in the vice, and use the bench plane to skim off the pencilled marks – so that the waste comes away as three short shavings. Take another sighting, pencil the high spots, and repeat the planing.

Continue sighting, marking, and planing until the three shavings get longer and longer, to the point where they come away as a single board-length shaving (step 1). Lay out the width of the side board from the planed edge, and then plane the opposite edge down to the gauged mark.

Shearing the end grain with the bench plane

Take the boards – all painstakingly faced on sides and edges – and carefully measure, square, and cut all the boards to about ½ in over the true finished length. Within this length, mark out the sawn boards at 70 in, and the six shelf boards at 11 in. One piece at a time, secure the wood (end grain uppermost) in the vise, and clamp a strip of waste to the far edge

of the wood – meaning at the plane exit-end of the run. Set the bench plane on the surface to be worked, just as if you were going to plane it straight on, then turn the plane at a slightly skewed angle and make the first shearing pass. Make repeated passes until tests with the square confirm that the surface is down to the mark and true (step 2).

Setting out the design

Select one long board and, starting at the "top", use the pencil, rule and square to set out the board with step-offs at 5 in, and then 1½ in, 10 in, 1½ in, 10 in, 1½ in and so on along the length of the wood. Square the lines around to both sides of the wood. Continue until you have established the position of all six shelves (step 3). Run a center line along the length of the 1½ in step-off, and fix the position of the dowel centers by measuring in 1½ in from each edge of the board. Transfer all the measurements through to the other board. Take the six shelves, run center lines along the end-grain edges, and mark the position of the dowel holes 1½ in in from the side of the board.

Drilling the holes

Take the side board and, making sure that you protect it with pieces of waste, clamp it in position on the drill-press table – so that one or other of the hole centers is aligned with the drill. Having first checked that the drill bit and the dowel match up, run the hole through the thickness of the wood (step 4).

Rerun this procedure with all the holes on both lengths of wood. When you come to drilling the holes into the ends of the shelves, you will need to work out a clamp-and-block system for holding the wood square and at the right height (step 5). The holes need to be 1½ in deep.

Assembly and finishing

Have a dry run put-together to make sure that the structure is square, then smear a small amount of glue on mating surfaces – on the butt joints, in the holes, and around the dowels – tap the dowels home (step 6), and clamp up. When the glue is dry, sand down all the surfaces to a smooth finish. Give all the surfaces a thin coat of Danish oil, allow to dry, and then burnish with beeswax and a soft cloth.

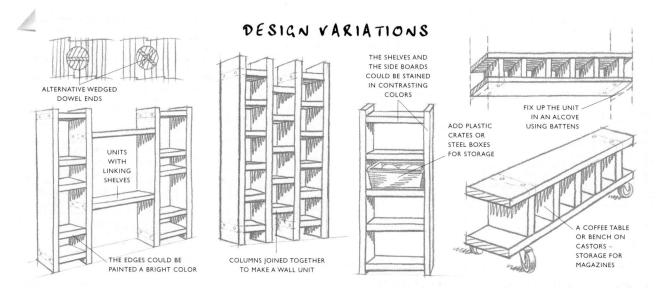

DESIGN VARIATIONS

ALTERNATIVE WEDGED DOWEL ENDS

UNITS WITH LINKING SHELVES

THE EDGES COULD BE PAINTED A BRIGHT COLOR

COLUMNS JOINED TOGETHER TO MAKE A WALL UNIT

THE SHELVES AND THE SIDE BOARDS COULD BE STAINED IN CONTRASTING COLORS

ADD PLASTIC CRATES OR STEEL BOXES FOR STORAGE

FIX UP THE UNIT IN AN ALCOVE USING BATTENS

A COFFEE TABLE OR BENCH ON CASTORS – STORAGE FOR MAGAZINES

MAKING THE COLUMN BOOKCASE

Planing the edges
Use the bench plane to straighten the edges of all the boards. Make repeated passes until the waste comes out as a continuous board-length ribbon.

2 Testing for squareness
Use a square to check that the ends of all the boards are correctly planed.

3 Marking the shelf positions
Hold the square firm and draw the line around both sides of the side board.

4 Drilling the side boards
Clamp the side board in position, check that the forstner drill bit is perfectly centered on the guide lines, and bore the dowel hole through.

5 Drilling the shelves
Clamp the board in position and make sure that it is square in both the horizontal and vertical planes. Drill the dowel holes to a depth of 1½ in.

6 Knocking in the dowels
Protect the workpiece with a scrap of wood, and tap the dowel into place.

TROUBLESHOOTING

- If you do decide to reduce the making time by getting the wood planed to thickness and cut to length, then make allowances for mistakes by having each piece at least 1 in overlength.

- You will need help at the drilling stage – to lift and hold the side boards in position.

2: FOLK ART SHELF

The wonderful thing about this little, folk art pine shelf – a characteristic of its type – is its uninhibited freshness. It isn't weighed down with curlicues, or in any way pretending to be what it's not, it is simply a stylish and functional hat and coat rack with whittled pegs.

CUTTING LIST

part	quantity	L x W x T
pine shelf board	1	35 x 9¼ x ¾
pine wall board	1	35 x 9 x ¾
pine brackets	2	9 x 9 x ⅛
pine pegs	4	5¼ x 1⅛ x ¾

(finished sizes, given in inches)

As with most folk art woodwork, it's beautifully easy to build – no difficult joints or complex finishes, you simply butt the component parts together, fit them with screws and dowels, and give the whole piece a color wash, topped off with wax.

Considering the design

Look at the working drawings and notes. This is a basic, swift-to-make structure – just a wall board, a shelf supported by two brackets, and three whittled pegs – all made of pine.

Certainly the fretted shape does need some careful setting out with a compass, and the pegs do need to be whittled with a knife, but, that apart, this is undoubtedly one of the easiest projects in the book. And, of course, if you like the overall idea of the project but aren't so keen on whittling, or you want the design of the wall board and brackets to reflect the quarter-circle of the shelf, then the design can easily be changed. As for the color, we have

TOOLS AND MATERIALS

- band saw or rip saw, or pre-sawn lumber
- crosscut saw
- power scroll saw (or hand coping saw)
- bench plane and block plane
- brace with bits at ⅜ in and ¾ in
- utility knife or Swedish sloyd knife
- selection of clamps
- square, compass, rule, and pencil
- graded sandpaper
- PVA glue and masking tape
- artists' watercolor paint (color to suit)
- Danish oil and beeswax polish
- 4 x dowels ⅜ in diameter, 2 in long
- 4 x screws 1¼ in long
- pine (see cutting list)

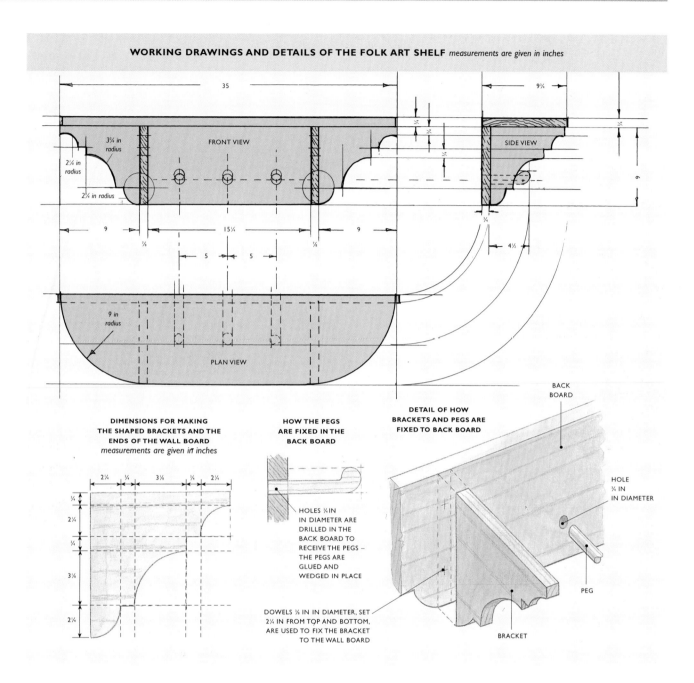

WORKING DRAWINGS AND DETAILS OF THE FOLK ART SHELF *measurements are given in inches*

FRONT VIEW

SIDE VIEW

PLAN VIEW

9 in radius

3¼ in radius

2¼ in radius

2¼ in radius

DIMENSIONS FOR MAKING THE SHAPED BRACKETS AND THE ENDS OF THE WALL BOARD
measurements are given in inches

HOW THE PEGS ARE FIXED IN THE BACK BOARD

HOLES ¼ IN IN DIAMETER ARE DRILLED IN THE BACK BOARD TO RECEIVE THE PEGS – THE PEGS ARE GLUED AND WEDGED IN PLACE

DOWELS ⅛ IN IN DIAMETER, SET 2¼ IN FROM TOP AND BOTTOM, ARE USED TO FIX THE BRACKET TO THE WALL BOARD

DETAIL OF HOW BRACKETS AND PEGS ARE FIXED TO BACK BOARD

BACK BOARD

HOLE ¼ IN IN DIAMETER

PEG

BRACKET

chosen a hot American red to suit the theme of our own little garden summerhouse, but you could just as well select a sharp, Mediterranean blue, dappled green, or whatever color takes your fancy.

Preparing the wood

Having checked the wood at the time of purchase – to avoid faults – recheck to ensure that the sawn wood is free from shrinkage splits. Pay particular attention to the ends of the wall board, and to the two brackets. On no account must the brackets show splits along the run of the grain.

Plane the wood down to thickness – ¾ in and ⅞ in as indicated – and mark the best face. Arrange the brackets so that the grain runs horizontally from front to back, and use a crosscut saw to cut the four components to length: the shelf, the wall board, and the two bracket pieces.

Setting out the design details

First use the rule, square, and compass to work out the design on paper – so that you know precisely how the various curves and steps relate to the width and grain of your wood. When you are satisfied with this trial run, then mark out the "step-and-curve" design on the two brackets and the ends of the wall board (step 1, see over page). Shade in the areas to the waste side of the drawn lines. Set the compass to a radius of 9 in, and scribe out the shelf with the curve of the quarter-circle. Use the square to mark the position of the brackets on the front of the wall board and on the underside of the shelf.

Cutting the steps and curves

Check the shape of the drawn profiles against the detail drawing – both brackets should be identical and a good fit on the ends of the wall board – and then set to work cutting the four profiles. If you work at a slow pace, all the while making sure that the blade is presented with the line of the next cut, the sawn edges will finish up so smooth that they hardly need to be sanded (step 2).

Drilling the holes

Look at the working drawings and the step photographs opposite, and note that there are two dowel holes on

each bracket, and four dowel and three peg holes on the wall board, with the dowel holes being ⅜ in diameter and the peg holes ¾ in.

Establish the position of the holes with center points and sink them with the brace and the ⅜ in/¾ in bits. Ensure that the bracket holes are square and to the correct depth by clamping down the paired brackets flat on the bench and using a depth stop – a strip of masking tape wrapped around the drill bit – to gauge the hole depth (step 3). Drill the holes in the brackets – to a depth of 1⅜ in – and use them to transfer the position of the dowel holes through to the wall board (step 4).

Making the pegs

Draw out the shape of the pegs on tracing paper, and transfer the drawn lines through to the chosen pieces of wood. Set out four pegs so that you

have a spare. Shade in on the waste side of the drawn line and cut out the shapes on the scroll saw (step 5).

Start the modeling by whittling down the end of the peg with the knife, so that it is a push-fit in a ¾ in diameter hole. Socket the peg in a piece of scrap and then gradually shave away the sharp edges until it takes on a nicely rounded shape (step 6). Work with a tight, apple-paring stroke, all the while being ready to stop if you feel the knife slipping out of control. Stand the component parts of the shelf together and see how the pegs look in context.

Assembly

When you have modeled the pegs to shape, and had a trial fitting, next comes the slightly tricky procedure of fixing the brackets in place with the dowels. The order of work is as follows: screw the shelf to the top edge of the wall board using 1¼ in screws, glue the dowels in the wall board, locate the brackets on the dowels (step 7), glue the pegs in place (step 8), and then finally clamp up.

Finishing

When you are happy with the way that the shelf has come together, give the whole piece a rub down with the graded sandpaper – so that all surfaces are smooth to the touch. Clean away the dust and debris, and move to a dust-free area. Mix your chosen paint with water and lay on the resultant wash in repeated thin coats until you have a pleasing density of color. Finally, rub through the paint on selected edges and corners with medium-grade sandpaper. Give the whole piece a thin coat of Danish oil, burnish with beeswax polish, and the shelf is ready for hanging.

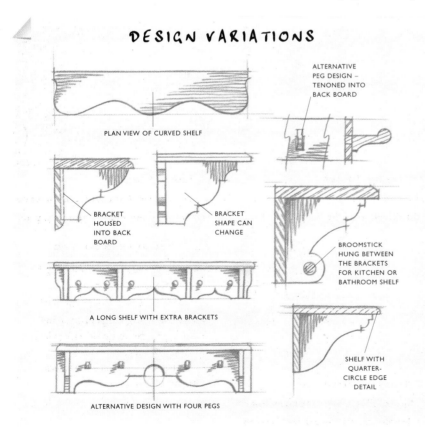

DESIGN VARIATIONS

PLAN VIEW OF CURVED SHELF

ALTERNATIVE PEG DESIGN – TENONED INTO BACK BOARD

BRACKET HOUSED INTO BACK BOARD

BRACKET SHAPE CAN CHANGE

BROOMSTICK HUNG BETWEEN THE BRACKETS FOR KITCHEN OR BATHROOM SHELF

A LONG SHELF WITH EXTRA BRACKETS

SHELF WITH QUARTER-CIRCLE EDGE DETAIL

ALTERNATIVE DESIGN WITH FOUR PEGS

MAKING THE FOLK ART SHELF

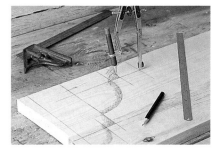

1 Setting out the stepped design
Use the compass to mark the "step-and-curve" design on the wall board.

2 Fretting out the brackets
Cut out the brackets on the scroll saw – so that the edges are left smooth.

3 Drilling the brackets
Clamp the brackets secure, align the drill to both the floor and the bench, and run the holes in to the depth of the masking-tape stop.

4 Positioning the dowel holes
Prop the shelf and the wall board together at right angles, and use the holes in the drilled bracket to mark off the position of the dowel holes.

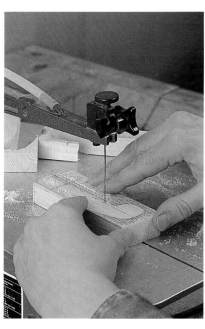

5 Cutting the pegs
Cut the pegs out on the scroll saw. Advance the workpiece at a steady rate – so that the blade is to the waste side of the drawn line.

6 Carving the pegs
Carve the top of the peg by cutting in the direction of the holding block.

7 Gluing the brackets
Spread **PVA** glue in the holes, insert the dowels, and set the bracket in place.

8 Gluing the pegs
Smear glue in the hole, push the peg into position, and wipe away excess glue.

TROUBLESHOOTING

- You could miss out the whittling by using old, cast iron or brass coat pegs – easily found at garage sales.
- There are several options for the color; you can use children's paints mixed with water, artists' watercolors, or even water-based household paint.

3: RIETVELD "CRATE" BOOKCASE

If you are looking to build the most basic of bookcases – and we really do mean basic – then you can't do better than a classic, Rietveld "crate" design. Crate or *krat* furniture had its beginnings in the 1930s Depression, when Gerrit Rietveld, the Dutch cabinetmaker, designed a system of low-cost furniture.

TOOLS AND MATERIALS

- band saw, thicknesser, surface planer (or use pre-milled lumber – see Tools, Techniques, and Materials, page 12)
- crosscut saw
- backsaw
- clamps and scrap wood to make a jig
- bench drill (or brace), hand-held power drill, drill bits ⅜ in and 5/16 in diameter
- square, rule, dividers, marking gauge, marking knife, awl, pencil
- bench plane and block plane
- toggle hardware: 20 x 6M brass hex heads, 20 x 6M ¾ in toggles, and 20 x 2½ in lengths of 6M threaded rod
- 16 x brass countersunk no. 8 screws
- screwdriver and key to fit the brass hex heads
- wire brush and fine sandpaper
- Danish oil and beeswax polish
- American oak (see cutting list)

CUTTING LIST

part	quantity	L x W x T
oak end boards	2	49 x 140 x ⅞
oak vertical back boards	2	34 x 140 x ⅞
oak shelves	4	38¼ x 140 x ⅞
oak kick board	1	38¼ x 153 x ⅞

(finished sizes, given in inches)

Gerrit Rietveld came up with the notion that an unskilled public could make furniture from wood salvaged from packing cases. What could be easier? No complex joints, just planks and a handful of screws and bolts, and you are on your way to building a classic designer bookcase.

Considering the design

Look at the working drawings and step-by-step photographs, and consider how the crate system uses pre-milled planks as a basic building module. The planks are butted top to side and fixed with toggle bolts and screws, with the two back boards and the single kick board being used to stabilize the structure. Note how the two back boards are cut short to allow for the baseboard – so that the shelves sit flush to the wall.

Planing the face edge

Take the nine lengths of carefully chosen wood, and check them over to make sure that they are free from splits and knots. First plane all the wood down to a uniform thickness of ⅞ in, then, one plank at a time, mount

WORKING DRAWINGS AND DETAILS OF THE RIETVELD "CRATE" BOOKCASE *measurements are given in inches*

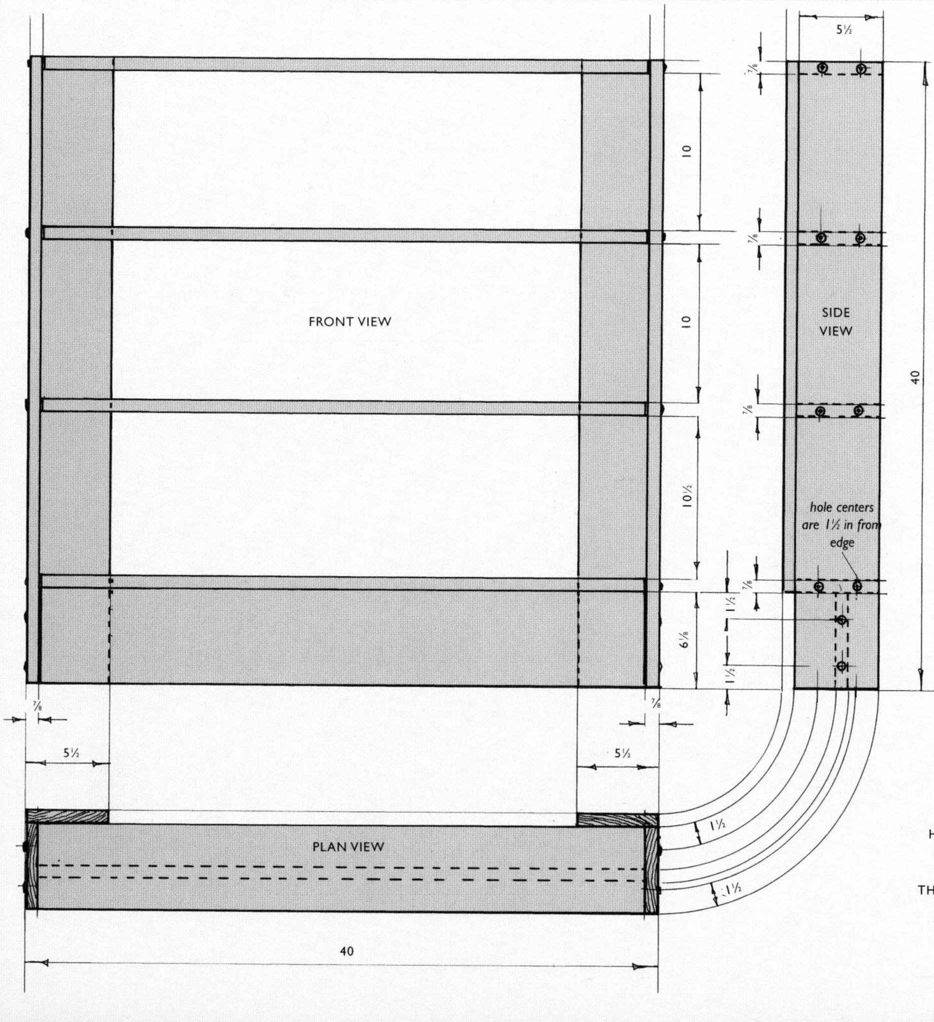

FRONT VIEW
SIDE VIEW
PLAN VIEW
5½
⅞
10
10
10½
6⅞
1½
40
hole centers are 1½ in from edge
1½
5½
5½
⅞
40

DETAIL OF HOW THE PLANKS ARE FIXED TOGETHER AT THE TOP OF THE UNIT

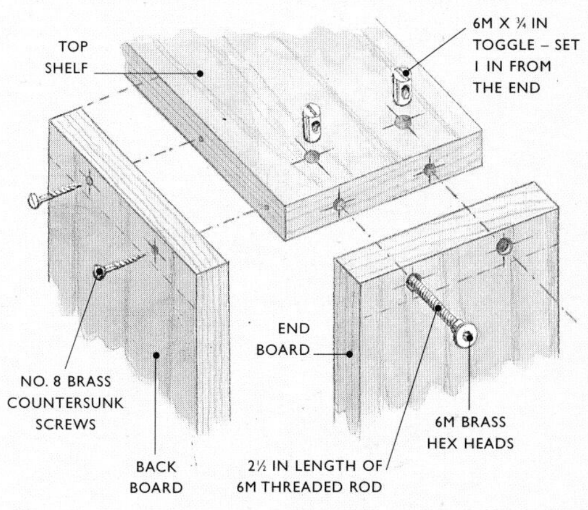

TOP SHELF
6M X ¾ IN TOGGLE – SET 1 IN FROM THE END
END BOARD
NO. 8 BRASS COUNTERSUNK SCREWS
BACK BOARD
2½ IN LENGTH OF 6M THREADED ROD
6M BRASS HEX HEADS

CROSS-SECTION DETAIL OF THE FIXINGS USED TO JOIN THE ENDS OF THE SHELVES TO THE END BOARDS AND KICK BOARD

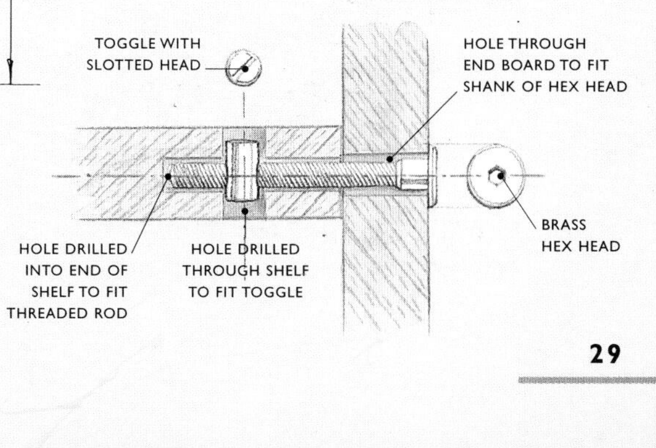

TOGGLE WITH SLOTTED HEAD
HOLE THROUGH END BOARD TO FIT SHANK OF HEX HEAD
BRASS HEX HEAD
HOLE DRILLED INTO END OF SHELF TO FIT THREADED ROD
HOLE DRILLED THROUGH SHELF TO FIT TOGGLE

the wood low down in the vise and use a bench plane to work the face edge to a square finish. This done, set the gauge to the appropriate width measurement and run a line round the wood. Finally, shade in the waste, mount the wood in the vise, set the plane to take the finest cut, and gradually plane down to the gauged line (step 1).

Planing the end grain

Measure about ¼ in along from one end of the plank, slide the try square up to the mark, and use a knife to square the mark around the wood. Measure the length along from the squared line and repeat the procedure on the other end.

Use a bench hook and the backsaw to cut the wood to length – with the line of cut being on the waste side of the marked line. Secure the workpiece in the vise and plane the end grain to a smooth finish (step 2).

Marking out

Look at the working drawings and details, and consider how the toggle hole centers are always set 1½ in in from the side edge of the board and 1 in along from the end, with the threaded rod running into the center of the plank thickness.

To mark out, establish the position of the two boards that go to make the joint, lay out the lines with a pencil and square, fix the position of the various holes, and then punch in the hole centers with the awl (step 3).

Drilling

Starting with holes that run through the thickness of the boards, set the workpiece in a simple jig – two battens at right angles screwed to a base board. Move the jig around on the drill-press table until the bit is on target, clamp the jig in place, and run the hole through with the ⅜ in bit (step 4).

When you have finished all the through-board holes, take the square and pencil, and run guidelines from the hole centers and over the end of the board. Check it all, then position the board in the vise – at a comfortable height, and so that you can sight down the lines – and use the power drill to sink the holes (step 5).

Finishing

Take your wire brush – either a hand brush, or a rotary brush fitted in a power drill – and stroke the wood vigorously in the direction of the grain. Pay particular attention to the top face of the top shelf, the outside of the end boards, the edges as seen in front view, and the end grain as seen in the plan view. Finally, when you have sculpted the grain to your liking, clean away the dust and debris, wipe all the surfaces over with a thin coat of Danish oil, allow to dry, and then burnish with beeswax.

Assembly

When you have completed the nine boards – all drilled, wire-brushed, oiled, and waxed – you must fix them together with the toggles. To do this, screw a brass hex head on to one end of a 2½ in length of thread, and slide the thread through the thickness of one board and on into the end-grain hole of another.

Set the toggle in place with the screwdriver slot uppermost, turn the brass head until the threaded rod engages with the toggle, and tighten up with the key until the two boards are drawn together and clenched tight (step 6). Finally, give all the surfaces a burnishing with wax.

DESIGN VARIATIONS

SHELVES TO DISPLAY SMALL OBJECTS

BACK BOARDS EXTENDED TO MAKE HANGING SHELVES

TALLER DESIGN TO FIT A NARROW SPACE

CENTER SHELVES ARE STAGGERED TO ACCOMMODATE HARDWARE

LONG TOP LINKING TWO UNITS

EXTENDED TOP

LOW FREE-STANDING SHELF USING PAIRS OF BOARDS

MAKING THE RIETVELD "CRATE" BOOKCASE

1 Planing all the edges
Use a bench plane to plane the edges of the boards. Use your fingers to ensure that the plane is held square to the face of the wood.

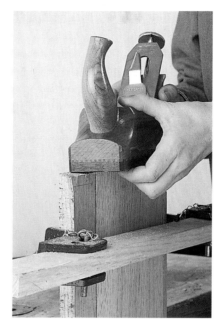

2 Planing the end grain
Use a bench plane to clean up the ends of all the boards. Clamp a waste block against the workpiece to avoid splitting the end grain.

3 Marking out the holes
Carefully set out the position of the fixing holes with the dividers and the square. Spike the centers of the holes with the awl.

4 Using the drilling jig
Butt the workpiece hard up against the fence, bring the bit slowly down on target, and then sink the hole. Work at a leisurely pace to avoid exit damage.

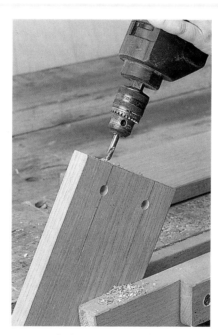

5 Drilling the ends of the boards
Use a power drill to make the holes in the ends of the shelves and the kick board. Adjust the angle of approach so that these holes are perfectly aligned.

6 Assembling
Tighten the brass hex head and toggle hardware with the key.

TROUBLESHOOTING

- It is vital when making a jig to double-check the measurements – it is a good idea to make a couple of test runs with scrap wood.

- If by chance you leave a burr on the end of the threaded rod, and the toggle and/or brass head refuses to engage, then use a file to tidy up the end of the thread.

4: CUBE BOOKCASE

The design of this bookcase addresses the problem of how best, in a relatively small space, to store and present a good number of different sized items – books, CDs, rolls of paper, and the like – when the items variously need to be seen in either landscape or portrait alignment.

TOOLS AND MATERIALS

- band saw, or pre-milled lumber
- crosscut saw and gents saw
- bench and block planes
- bench drill (or brace)
- forstner drill bits: ⅜ in, ½ in and ¾ in diameter
- square, dividers, rule, and pencil
- marking knife
- single-pin marking gauge
- bevel-edge chisels: ½ in and ¾ in wide
- graded sandpaper
- PVA glue and 1 in brads
- two brass hanging plates
- green, water-base, felt-tip pen
- Danish oil and beeswax polish
- 24 x dowels, ⁵⁄₁₆ in diameter, 1½ in long
- maple (see cutting list)

CUTTING LIST

part	quantity	L x W x T
maple boards 'A'	3	37½ x 6⅛ x ¾
maple boards 'B'	2	39 x 6⅛ x ¾
maple boards 'C'	2	18½ x 6⅛ x ¾
maple boards 'D'	4	18⅝ x 6 x ½
maple boards 'E'	4	9⅛ x 6 x ½

(finished sizes, given in inches)

Boards 'A' to 'E' refer to working drawing

The cube bookcase draws its inspiration from 1950s Swedish furniture – the type of "pigeon-hole" cabinets that were used in offices for holding books and stationery. All we did here was to play around with the square module theme, color the face edge, and… the cube design was born.

Considering the design

Look at the working drawings and notes. Consider how the form calls for a fair degree of precise measuring and cutting. It's not so much that the joints are complex – they are in fact no more than a mix of basic dado joints and dowels – but rather it is that the square module draws attention to small mistakes – with the success of the project hinging on the elements being absolutely square and true, the design calls for a high degree of accuracy at both the laying out and cutting stages. As to the choice of wood, it is best to choose a light-colored wood like birch, beech, or maple. These woods are knot-free with a uniform texture.

WORKING DRAWINGS AND DETAIL OF THE CUBE BOOKCASE *measurements are given in inches*

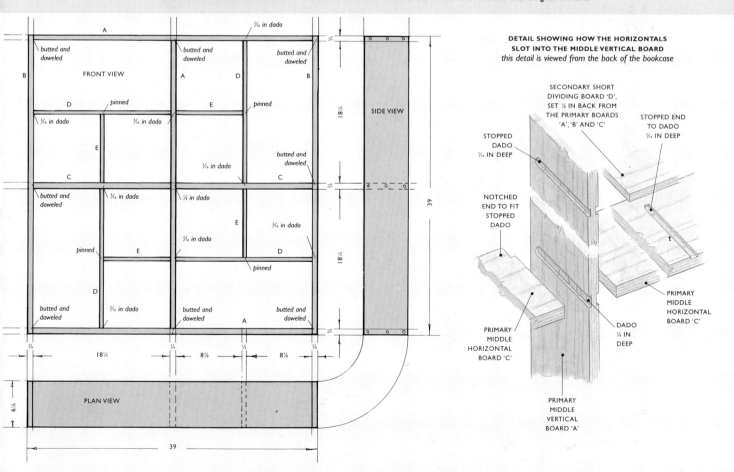

DETAIL SHOWING HOW THE HORIZONTALS SLOT INTO THE MIDDLE VERTICAL BOARD
this detail is viewed from the back of the bookcase

Preparing the wood

Take the fifteen boards – the top and bottom boards, the side and middle vertical boards, the two middle horizontal boards, the four long dividing boards, and the four short dividing boards – and check them over to make sure that they are free from knots, splits, and stains. Plane the boards to thickness and width, and pencil-mark face side and face edge.

Setting out the joints

Allow $\frac{1}{16}$ in of extra wood each end for the make-up of the joints, cut the boards to length, plane the ends square and true, and write in pencil on each board so that you know its placing and position. Label mating boards and joints.

Being mindful that you are dealing with two thicknesses of wood – $\frac{3}{4}$ in for the outside frame and the primary cross-members, and $\frac{1}{2}$ in for the secondary members – use the rule, dividers, and square to set out the dados (step 1). It has to be right the first time around, so spend time double-checking that all is correct.

Cutting the housings

Set out the housings at $\frac{1}{4}$ in and $\frac{3}{16}$ in deep – see working drawing. Use the $\frac{3}{4}$ in and the $\frac{1}{2}$ in drills respectively to sink flat-bottomed holes at the stopped ends. Sink the holes to the depth of the dado.

Score in the drawn lines with a knife and chisel to the waste side of the cuts – so that you have two beveled guide tracks for the saw. Saw down to just short of the depth of the flat-bottomed hole (step 2), and clear the resultant waste with a chisel (step 3). Make depth checks to ensure that you don't cut too deep (step 4). Use one of the shelves to check for width.

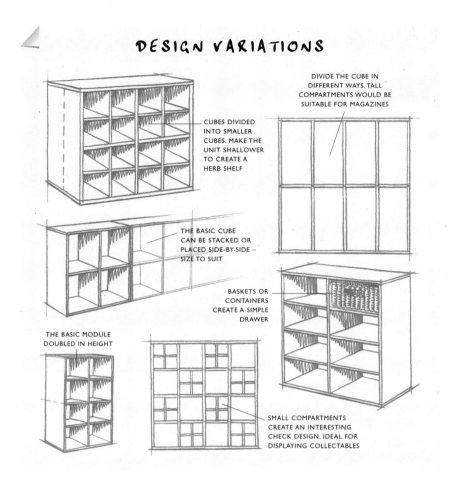

DESIGN VARIATIONS

DIVIDE THE CUBE IN DIFFERENT WAYS. TALL COMPARTMENTS WOULD BE SUITABLE FOR MAGAZINES

CUBES DIVIDED INTO SMALLER CUBES. MAKE THE UNIT SHALLOWER TO CREATE A HERB SHELF

THE BASIC CUBE CAN BE STACKED OR PLACED SIDE-BY-SIDE – SIZE TO SUIT

BASKETS OR CONTAINERS CREATE A SIMPLE DRAWER

THE BASIC MODULE DOUBLED IN HEIGHT

SMALL COMPARTMENTS CREATE AN INTERESTING CHECK DESIGN, IDEAL FOR DISPLAYING COLLECTABLES

Completing the joints

When you are happy with the fit and finish of individual dados, set out the components on the bench, and have a trial fitting. Modify and adjust the depth of the dados so that the structure comes together for a good, close fit. Study the design and see how the secondary divisions (boards 'D' and 'E') are set $\frac{1}{16}$ in back from the primary frame. Use a pencil, rule, and square to set out the front-of-shelf notches. Cut the waste back with the gents saw – with the depth of the notches being equal to the depth that the secondary members are set back. Plane the edges to reduce the width.

Assembly

Clamp the primary members together and dry-fit with three dowels at each outer corner. Check with the square and make any necessary adjustments. Have a trial dry run and decide on the working order of the glue-up (step 5), having first prepared the clamps, made sure that you have enough glue, and have generally cleared the decks for the task ahead. Smear glue on mating surfaces, brad and clamp up.

Finishing

When the glue is completely dry, rub down all the surfaces to a smooth finish. Be sure to sand in the direction of the grain. Color the selected face edges with the felt-tip pen (step 6). Rub through the color to enhance the grain, and give all the surfaces a thin coat of Danish oil. Sand down the grain, burnish the finished piece with beeswax, and finally screw the two brass hanging plates in position on the back edges of the side boards.

MAKING THE CUBE BOOKCASE

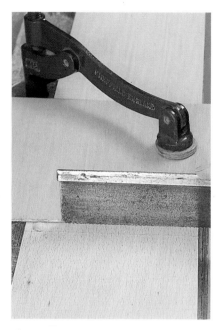

1 Setting out the dados

Use the square to mark the various housings – ¼ in wide for the outside frame and the primary cross-members, and ½ in for all the others.

2 Sawing the dados

Clamp a thin strip of plywood to the side of the line of cut, to help keep the saw on track, and run the saw cut down to the depth of the drilled hole.

3 Chiseling the dados

Use a bevel-edge chisel to remove the waste. Hold the chisel flat against the wood, and gradually pare down to the desired depth.

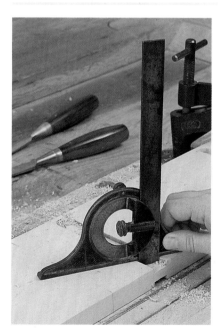

6 Coloring the edges

Use a felt-tip pen to color the face edges – as shown in the project picture.

TROUBLESHOOTING

- Some woodworkers like to cut stopped dados by first drilling the flat-bottomed hole, and then squaring the hole with a chisel to make room for the leading end of the saw.

- If by chance you cut one of the dados too deep, make good by packing up the bottom with veneer.

4 Checking the dado depth

Use the end of the adjustable square to ensure that the dados are at the correct depth – ¼ in or ³⁄₁₆ in deep (see the working drawings).

5 Assembling

Have a trial fitting and delicately pencil in necessary registration marks. Decide on the clamp arrangement and order of assembly, and then glue up.

5: DOUBLE-BRACKET SLAT SHELF

We were sitting in our sun room, soaking up the sunshine, and musing about how we were going to fill the room with potted plants, when it came to us that what the room really needed was lots of super-strong, open-slat shelves. This early twentieth century summerhouse design fits the bill perfectly.

TOOLS AND MATERIALS

- rip saw, band saw, or pre-milled lumber
- crosscut saw
- backsaw and gents saw
- scroll saw (or hand coping saw)
- marking gauge
- bench plane and block plane
- selection of bevel-edge paring chisels
- mortise gauge
- selection of clamps, including a bar clamp
- square, dividers or compass, rule and pencil
- 20 x screws 1¼ in long and 6 hooks
- power sander and graded sandpaper
- Danish oil
- pine (see cutting list)

CUTTING LIST

part	quantity	L x W x T
pine slats	5	36 x 1½ x ¾
pine back boards	2	11½ x 4⅜ x ¾
pine bearers and uprights	8	12 x 3 x ¾
(finished sizes, given in inches)		

The double-bracket design makes it strong enough to take the heaviest pots, the slats are spaced so as to give it a light and airy feel, and the brass hooks are good for hanging summerhouse paraphernalia.

Considering the design

Study the working drawings, and observe how the double-bracket arrangement with the slot mortise and the dovetail joints give it a great deal of strength, yet the structure isn't in any way overpowering or heavy. Note how the dovetail pin runs through the slot mortise to lock the bearer and the upright together in such a way as to prevent the double brackets from skewing and pulling apart. The design is perfectly suited to its purpose of carrying heavy weights, in that it allows for the shelf to be hung with hardware running through both the uprights and the back board. If you are worried about the strength of the shelf, you can have eight screws – two through each back board, and one through each of the four bracket risers.

Preparing the wood

If, like me, you have chosen to use low-cost pine, you will need to arrange the wood so that the knots

WORKING DRAWINGS AND DETAIL OF THE DOUBLE-BRACKET SLAT SHELF *measurements are given in inches*

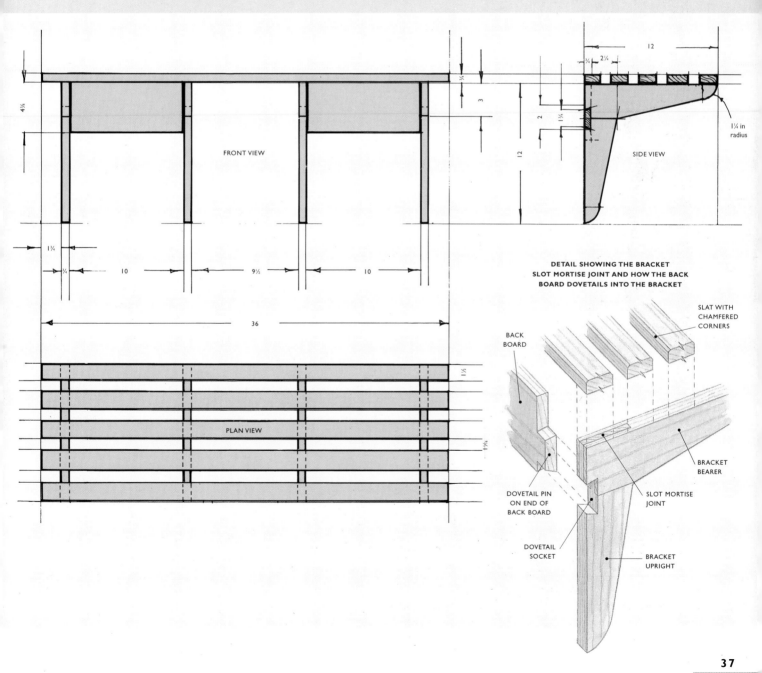

FRONT VIEW

SIDE VIEW

1¼ in radius

PLAN VIEW

DETAIL SHOWING THE BRACKET
SLOT MORTISE JOINT AND HOW THE BACK
BOARD DOVETAILS INTO THE BRACKET

SLAT WITH CHAMFERED CORNERS

BACK BOARD

BRACKET BEARER

DOVETAIL PIN ON END OF BACK BOARD

SLOT MORTISE JOINT

DOVETAIL SOCKET

BRACKET UPRIGHT

are placed well clear of the joints. Plane down all the wood to a uniform thickness of ¾ in, and to the required widths. Measure and square the wood to length and cut it down into the component parts. You need five slats, two back boards, four bracket bearers, and four bracket uprights. Use the block plane to remove the sharp corners on the top edges of the slats, and to square the end grain to a good finish.

Making the joints

Note that the bearers and the uprights, that together make the brackets, are identical in size and shape – until they are jointed. Take the eight pieces of wood that you have chosen for the brackets, and use the rule, compass and square to set out the profile. Shade to the waste side of the drawn line and fret out the shape on the scroll saw (step 1).

Mark out the members of the slot mortise joints – four mortises and four tenons. Square the shoulder line around the wood. Set the gauge to just over one-third of the thickness, and mark the mortise and tenons over the end of the wood. They should look identical at this stage. Shade in the waste on all parts. Set the work in the vise and saw down to the squared shoulder line – with the line of the cut running to the waste side of the gauged line (step 2).

To cut the tenons, set the workpiece against the bench hook and saw down to the square line (step 3). To cut the mortises, set the workpiece in the vise and use a narrow-width chisel to pare down the waste level with the squared shoulder line (step 4). Fine-tune the components until the joint comes together for a tight push-fit, and then glue and clamp.

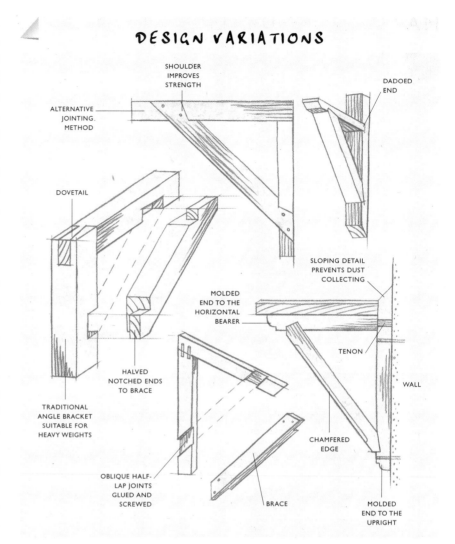

DESIGN VARIATIONS

SHOULDER IMPROVES STRENGTH

DADOED END

ALTERNATIVE JOINTING METHOD

DOVETAIL

SLOPING DETAIL PREVENTS DUST COLLECTING

MOLDED END TO THE HORIZONTAL BEARER

TENON

WALL

HALVED NOTCHED ENDS TO BRACE

TRADITIONAL ANGLE BRACKET SUITABLE FOR HEAVY WEIGHTS

CHAMFERED EDGE

OBLIQUE HALF-LAP JOINTS GLUED AND SCREWED

BRACE

MOLDED END TO THE UPRIGHT

Making the dovetail pin joints

Look at the working drawings. Note how, though this joint is termed a dovetail, it is in fact made up of a pin that slots into a dovetail socket, without there actually being a dovetail in sight. See also the way the joint is positioned with the express purpose of locking the joint.

Draw out the dovetail socket on the bracket, saw down the shoulder line, clear the bulk of the waste with the coping saw, and pare back the waste to the drawn line (step 5). Transfer the shape of the socket through to the ends of the back board, square in the shoulder line, and then use a small backsaw to clear the

waste at either side of the pin. Ease the pin until it is a good, tight fit in the socket (step 6). Glue and clamp the double bracket (step 7).

Assembly and finishing

Having made and glued the two double-bracket units and sanded them to a good finish, set them down on the bench and link them with the battens. Screw the first batten in place so that it is flush with the wall (step 8). Then set the other battens 1¹⁄₁₆ in apart – so that the last batten finishes flush with the front end of the bearer. Finally, rub down the piece to a smooth finish, and give all the surfaces a thin coat of Danish oil.

MAKING THE DOUBLE-BRACKET SLAT SHELF

1 Fretting the brackets
Fret out the bracket parts on the scroll saw – so that you have eight identical component parts: four uprights and four bearers.

2 Sawing the mortises
Use the backsaw to cut down to the shoulder line.

3 Cutting the tenons
Remove the waste from the cheeks of the tenons using the gents saw.

4 Clearing the mortise waste
Set the wood at an angle in the vise, and use the chisel to pare the waste from the slot mortise. Work from both sides to avoid exit damage.

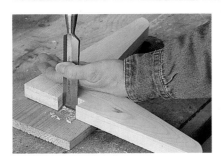

5 Cutting the dovetail
Use the chisel to pare back the waste to the gauged line.

6 Fitting the bracket dovetails
Cut the pin so that the dovetail is a tight push-fit.

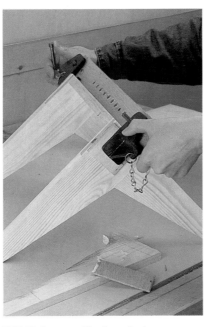

7 Gluing up the brackets
Spread glue inside the dovetail joints, put waste wood between the bar clamp and the workpiece, and tighten up. Check for squareness.

8 Assembling
Set the brackets 1¾ in from the ends of the batten and fix with screws.

TROUBLESHOOTING

- Be careful that you don't cut the joint too loose when you are cutting the components that make up the slot mortise joint. It is better to err towards over-tight and then ease back to a good fit.

- The dovetail needs to be a tight push-fit, with the pin centered on the shoulder line of the tenon.

6: AMERICAN ARTS AND CRAFTS BOOKCASE

This design is a tribute to **Gustav Stickley** – one of the leading lights of the American Arts and Crafts Movement. Stickley was, to our way of thinking, something of a misunderstood genius. The bold, direct style of his work perfectly manages to capture the spirit of the period just before the First World War.

TOOLS AND MATERIALS

- rip saw, band saw, or pre-milled lumber
- crosscut saw
- backsaw and gents saw
- scroll saw (or hand coping saw)
- marking gauge
- four planes: bench, block, rabbet and small bull-nose
- selection of bevel-edge paring chisels
- mortise gauge and marking knife
- square, dividers, rule, and pencil
- trammel
- 24 screws, 1 in long
- power sander and graded sandpaper
- Danish oil and beeswax polish
- American oak (see cutting list)

CUTTING LIST

part	quantity	L x W x T
oak side boards	2	56½ x 12 x ⅞
oak shelves	5	47¾ x 11½ x ¾
oak tongue-and-groove back boards to make up total area of:	1	50⅛ x 43½ x ½
oak wedges	8	3½ x ¾ x ½
(sizes given in inches)		

Made of oak with loose-wedge tenons, and with its reference to old-time ideals of thoroughness of workmanship, this bookcase draws its inspiration from the furniture designed and made by William Morris, Gustav Stickley, and Elbert Hubbard. We like to think of it as being "American homestead romantic."

Considering the design

Study the working drawings: this bookcase is quite a substantial piece – with many of the features of the Arts and Crafts Movement. The tops of the side boards are generously arched, the back is random tongue-and-grooved, the tenons are loose-wedged, the shelves are notched and dadoed into the side boards, and the whole structure has an air of dependability about it. It's a very stylish piece.

Preparing the wood

Check the wood for unacceptable knots and end splits, and plane it all down to thickness – ⅞ in for the side boards, ¾ in for the shelves, and ½ in for the back boards. Plane the wood to width – 12 in for the side boards, and 11½ in for the five shelves. Measure and square the wood to length and cut it down to size. Make a generous allowance for cutting waste.

You need nineteen boards in all – two side boards, three short shelves, two long shelves, and nine wide and three narrow back boards. Square up the sawn ends with the block plane, and pencil-mark the best face sides and edges – so that you know how each board is placed.

Setting out the side boards

Take the two side boards – both planed to size but generously over length – and run a center line down the length. Having measured and established the actual length, and the position of all five shelves within the length – with the three middle shelves

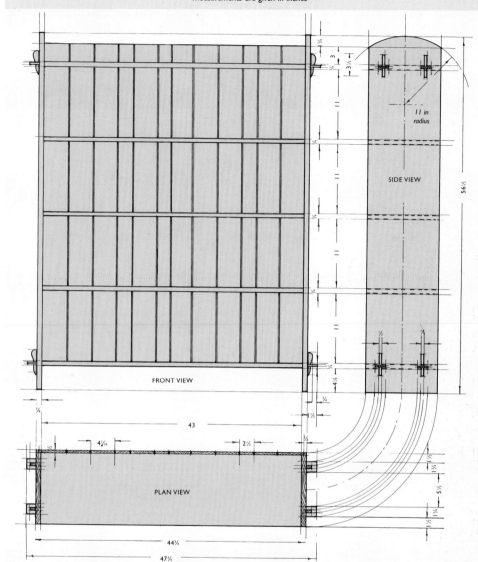

WORKING DRAWINGS AND DETAIL OF THE AMERICAN ARTS AND CRAFTS BOOKCASE
measurements are given in inches

SIDE VIEW

11 in radius

FRONT VIEW

PLAN VIEW

43

44¼

47¼

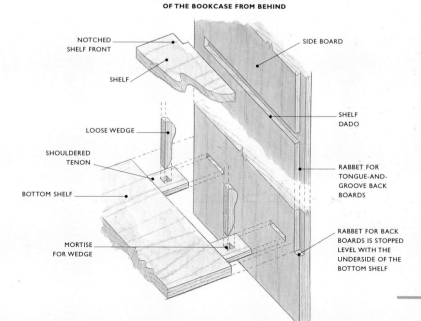

DETAIL OF THE LOWER CORNER OF THE BOOKCASE FROM BEHIND

NOTCHED SHELF FRONT

SHELF

LOOSE WEDGE

SHOULDERED TENON

BOTTOM SHELF

MORTISE FOR WEDGE

SIDE BOARD

SHELF DADO

RABBET FOR TONGUE-AND-GROOVE BACK BOARDS

RABBET FOR BACK BOARDS IS STOPPED LEVEL WITH THE UNDERSIDE OF THE BOTTOM SHELF being contained in stopped dados — square the lines around the sides and edges of the board, and draw in the position of the mortises. Shade the mortises into the waste side of the drawn lines. Set the trammel to a radius of 11 in, and run an arc across the width of the board (step 1).

Setting out the top and bottom shelves

Cut the two shelves to length at 47¾ in. Measure in from the ends of both boards and set out the tenons. Allow 1 in for the outer end of the tenon, ½ in for the wedge hole, and ⅞ in for the thickness of the side board — and square the measurement lines across the width. Shade the waste area (step 2). If you have managed to get the measurements right, the shoulder lines should end up 43 in apart.

Making the side boards

Take the two boards, with all the top curves and mortises clearly set out, and start by running a rabbet along the back inside face edge of the board — a rabbet stopped 4⅛ in short of the bottom end to take the tongue-and-groove boards. Set the gauge to ½ in, mark along the face of the board, and then secure the board down flat on the bench.

Take the rabbet plane, fit the blade in the forward position, set the fence to ½ in and the depth stop to ⅜ in, and work the rabbet from the top curve down to the stopped end. When the plane ceases to cut, to the point where the nose of the plane has come to a halt about ⅛ in from the stopped end, then remove the plane and use a chisel to pare the stopped end to a clean finish. Chop and pare through the mortises with the chisel

(step 3), cut the shelf dados as described in project 4, and cut and run the top curve with the coping saw and the block plane (step 4).

Cutting the double loose-wedged tenons

Having calculated and drawn out the double loose-wedged tenons on the ends of both planks, secure the board down flat on the bench, and chisel out the mortise so that the outermost face angles back slightly to accommodate the shape of the wedge. Set the workpiece in the vise, and run saw lines down on all four sides of both tenons to stop just short of the square shoulder line.

Use the coping saw to cut the waste from between the tenons, and then saw along the shoulder line to remove the remaining pieces of waste. Do this on the ends of both boards. Finally, reposition the workpiece in the vise and tidy up the shoulders and corners with the bull-nose plane (step 5). Avoid splitting the end grain.

Assembly

When you have finished the seven main boards — the two side boards with their rabbets and mortises, the

top and bottom shelves with their double loose-wedge tenons, and the three middle shelves all cut to fit with notches to the front edge — ease the top and bottom boards into place and set the piece face down on the bench. Slide the three middle shelves into their dados, and fit the tongue-and-groove boards into the rabbets and trim them to size (step 6). Adjust and ease the components until they come together for a square fit.

Making and fitting the wedges and finishing

Establish the shape of the wedge by making a single wedge to fit, and draw out eight identical profiles. Shade in on the waste side of the drawn line. Fret out the wedges on the scroll saw (step 7), and use a knife and sandpaper to bring them to a crisp, clean finish. Tap the wedges in place (step 8). Screw the tongue-and-groove back boards in place — use one screw per board at the bottom of the bookcase, and evenly distribute the rest. Finally, having rubbed down all the surfaces to a good, smooth finish, give all the surfaces a thin coat of Danish oil, and burnish the finished piece with beeswax polish.

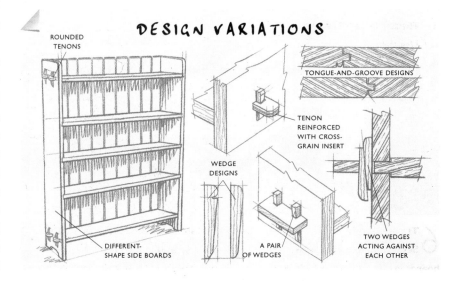

DESIGN VARIATIONS

ROUNDED TENONS

TONGUE-AND-GROOVE DESIGNS

TENON REINFORCED WITH CROSS-GRAIN INSERT

WEDGE DESIGNS

DIFFERENT-SHAPE SIDE BOARDS

A PAIR OF WEDGES

TWO WEDGES ACTING AGAINST EACH OTHER

MAKING THE ARTS AND CRAFTS BOOKCASE

1 Setting out the side boards
Set the trammel to 11 in, center the spike, and scribe the arc.

2 Setting out the shelf tenons
Set out the shape and position of the tenons with the square and rule.

3 Cutting the mortises
Use the bevel-edge chisel to pare the mortise holes to a clean-sided fit. Cut halfway through the thickness, and then work in from the other side.

4 Planing the top curve
Finish the curved shape with the block plane. Minimize the risk of splitting off the weak grain at the corners by working from side to middle.

5 Finishing the tenons
Use the bull-nose plane to clean up the shoulders of the tenons.

6 Trial assembly
Set the tongue-and-groove back boards in place and trim to length.

7 Cutting the wedges
Fret out the wedges on the scroll saw, and then sand to a good finish. Note how one side of the wedge uses the straight side edge of the wood.

8 Fitting the wedges
Gently tap the wedge in place to clench the joint.

TROUBLESHOOTING

- The trickiest part of this project is working all five shelves to a good fit. First make the side boards to fit the top and bottom shelves, and then finish by cutting the three middle shelves to fit the resultant width.

- Be careful that you don't weaken the wedge fitting by cutting the tenons too thin.

7: SHAKER HANGING SHELF

Made in pine and English beech, this intriguing little shelf is inspired by the hanging candle sconces made by the Shakers in their South Union Community in Kentucky in the late nineteenth century. The curious design has its roots in the Shaker belief that form follows function.

TOOLS AND MATERIALS

- band saw or rip saw, or pre-milled lumber
- crosscut saw
- scroll saw (or coping saw)
- bench plane and block plane
- bench drill (or brace)
- forstner drill bits: a large-diameter bit (1¹⁄₁₆ in) and a selection of smaller bits
- square, rule, gauge, compass, dividers, callipers, and pencil

- lathe with a selection of turning tools – gouges and scrapers
- large-size chisel for paring
- cabinet scraper
- PVA glue
- selection of screws and small nails
- power sander and graded sandpaper
- Danish oil and beeswax polish
- pine and English beech (see cutting list)

CUTTING LIST

part	quantity	L x W x T
pine shelf	1	36 x 6⅛ x ¾
pine T-square hangers	2	27½ x 12 x ¾
pine front brackets		
(cut from)	1	12 x 9 x ¾
pine peg board	1	33 x 2¾ x ¾
beech pegs and stops		
(cut from)	1	12 x 1½ x 1½

(finished sizes, given in inches)

The design is quite sophisticated, in that the peg-and-hole arrangement allows the shelf to be adjusted to suit your specific needs.

Considering the design

Look at the working drawings, and note how we have reduced the jointing to the minimum by cutting the T-square hanger from a single piece of wood, and by fixing the front brackets with screws rather than dowels. See also how the shelf is butt-jointed to both the bracket and the T-square hanger. As to the turnings – the mushroom pegs and the little knobs that distance the bottom of the T-square from the wall – they are turned all-of-a-piece as a spindle and then parted off with a saw. We chose pine for the overall structure, and easy-to-work beech for the turnings.

Preparing the wood

Plane down all your pine boards to a uniform thickness of ¾ in, square up the edges, and mark face sides and face edges. Consider how the forms are going to be set out, and generally make sure that critical areas – like around the bottom of the T-square hangers – are free from knots and splits. Take the square section length of wood that you have chosen for the turnings, and establish the end-centers by drawing crossed diagonals.

Setting out the design

Use a rule, square, and compass to set out the T-square hangers, the shelf with its rounded ends, and the peg board. To make the two front brackets, reduce the size of the basic fretted profile as indicated in the working drawing detail. Arrange the front brackets back-to-back on one piece of wood (step 1).

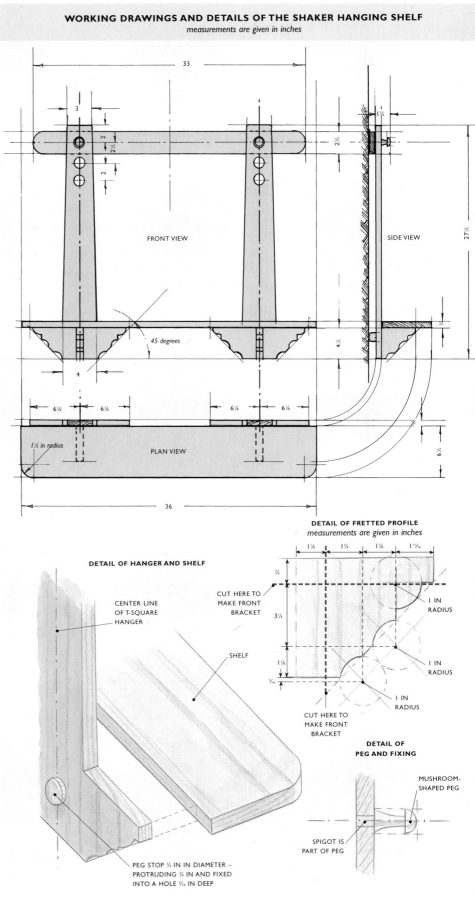

WORKING DRAWINGS AND DETAILS OF THE SHAKER HANGING SHELF
measurements are given in inches

FRONT VIEW

SIDE VIEW

45 degrees

PLAN VIEW

1½ in radius

DETAIL OF FRETTED PROFILE
measurements are given in inches

DETAIL OF HANGER AND SHELF

CENTER LINE OF T-SQUARE HANGER

SHELF

CUT HERE TO MAKE FRONT BRACKET

CUT HERE TO MAKE FRONT BRACKET

1 IN RADIUS

1 IN RADIUS

1 IN RADIUS

DETAIL OF PEG AND FIXING

MUSHROOM-SHAPED PEG

SPIGOT IS PART OF PEG

PEG STOP ¼ IN DIAMETER – PROTRUDING ¼ IN AND FIXED INTO A HOLE ⅜ IN DEEP

Fretting out the profiles

Check and carefully shade in the area to the waste side of the drawn lines – so that there is no doubting the precise line of cut. Ensure that the scroll saw is in good order, fit a new fine-tooth blade, and adjust the tension. Work at a slow, relaxed speed (step 2).

Boring the holes

There are sixteen holes in all – six large holes for hanging the shelf frame on the pegs, four holes for the front bracket screws, two holes for the stop knobs, two holes for fixing the peg spigots, and two holes in the peg board for the fixing screws.

The 1⅛ in holes are an important part of the design, so check that you have the appropriate bit sizes, and have a trial drilling to make sure that your bits are sharp enough to cut a clean, crisp-sided hole. When you have finished the large-diameter holes, wrap a sheet of fine-grade sandpaper around a piece of dowel offcut and rub down the edges of the holes to a slightly rounded finish (step 3).

Turning the pegs and stops

Take the square section of beech and mount it on the lathe. Turn the wood down to a smooth cylinder of 1 in diameter. Use the pencil and dividers to set out the cylinder with all the step-offs that make up the design. Allow ½ in for the heads, 1¼ in for the necks, ¾ in for the spiggots, ⅜ in for parting waste, and so on along the length of the wood.

Select a turning gouge, and turn the forms down to a fine finish. Check the diameters with the callipers (step 4), make necessary changes, and part off. Turn the peg stops in the same way (see the detail on page 45 for sizes).

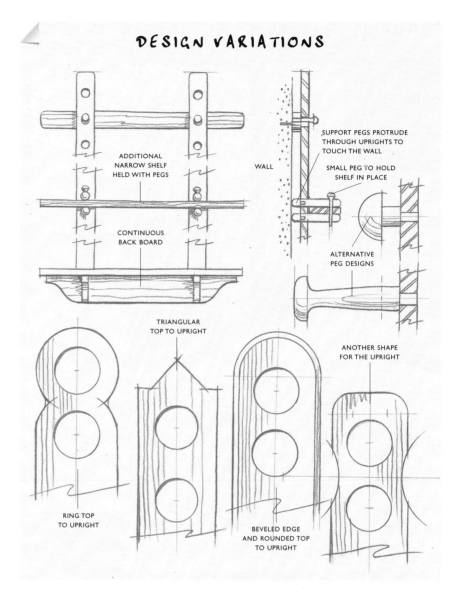

DESIGN VARIATIONS

ADDITIONAL NARROW SHELF HELD WITH PEGS

CONTINUOUS BACK BOARD

WALL

SUPPORT PEGS PROTRUDE THROUGH UPRIGHTS TO TOUCH THE WALL

SMALL PEG TO HOLD SHELF IN PLACE

ALTERNATIVE PEG DESIGNS

RING TOP TO UPRIGHT

TRIANGULAR TOP TO UPRIGHT

BEVELED EDGE AND ROUNDED TOP TO UPRIGHT

ANOTHER SHAPE FOR THE UPRIGHT

Assembly

When you have made all ten components that go to make up the design – the shelf, the two T-square hangers, the peg board, the two pegs, the two stops, and the two support brackets – then it is time to have a trial dry run put-together. Screw the two brackets in place (step 5), bridge the shelf across the brackets, make sure that the turnings socket into place, and use a measure and a square to generally make sure that all is correct. Having tried out each of the three shelf height positions, check for squareness and pencil in guide lines.

Finishing

When you are satisfied with the overall construction, disassemble the components and spend time bringing all the details to a good finish. Pare the ends of the peg board back to the scribed line (step 6), and glue the pegs and knobs in place (step 7). When you come to fitting the shelf board, first establish its precise position in relation to the brackets (step 8), and then glue and brad it into place.

Clean away the excess glue, sand to a smooth finish, and clean up the dust. Finally, give all surfaces a thin coat of Danish oil, and polish with beeswax.

MAKING THE SHAKER HANGING SHELF

Setting out the brackets
Use the compass to draw out the shapes of the brackets.

2 **Fretting the brackets**
Fret out the brackets on the scroll saw. Work to the waste side of the line.

3 **Sanding the peg holes**
Wrap sandpaper around a dowel and rub down the rim of the peg hole to a round-edge finish. Make sure the inside of the hole is smooth to the touch.

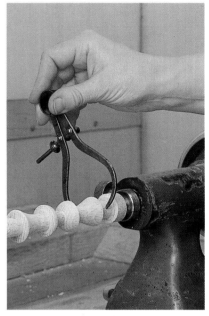

4 **Checking the peg diameters**
Turn the pegs on the lathe. Arrange them head to head, so that the two forms become a symmetrical whole. Use the callipers to check the diameters.

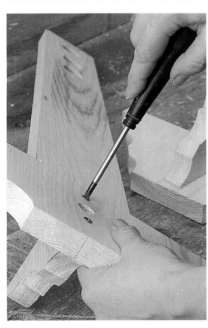

5 **Assembling the brackets**
To assemble the brackets, run in countersunk screws from the back of the T-square hangers, on into the brackets. Check for squareness.

6 **Paring the peg board**
Use the large-size chisel to pare the ends of the peg board to shape.

7 **Gluing the pegs**
Smear glue on mating surfaces and then push the peg home.

8 **Fitting the shelf**
Check the alignment of the shelf with the square, and mark the position.

TROUBLESHOOTING

- If you are working to a tight budget, you can – if you are very careful – cut the front brackets from waste left over from the T-square hangers.

- If you like the project but aren't so keen on the turning, then you can either buy the pegs ready-made, or you can whittle them to shape.

8: CYMA-CURVE HANGING SHELVES

This set of birch hanging shelves – an authentic copy of an original piece that was made in New England in the last quarter of the eighteenth century – is characterized by the graceful application of the decorative form known as the "cyma curve." An ideal piece of furniture for a small study.

TOOLS AND MATERIALS

- band saw or rip saw, or pre-milled lumber
- crosscut saw
- backsaw
- dovetail saw
- power scroll saw, or coping saw
- three planes: bench, block, and narrow "hollow" plane – about ¼ in wide at the cutting edge
- bench drill (or brace)
- single forstner drill bit, ½ in in diameter
- square, dividers, rule, and pencil
- marking knife
- large sheet of tracing paper – at least as big as one of the side boards
- single-brad marking gauge
- bevel-edge chisel about 1 in wide
- in-cannel or channel gouge with a sweep or curve to fit a circle with a diameter of ½ in
- power sander and graded sandpaper
- PVA glue
- selection of clamps
- two brass hanging plates
- Danish oil and beeswax polish
- European birch (see cutting list)

CUTTING LIST

part	quantity	L x W x T
birch top shelf	1	25⅛ x 5½ x ½
birch middle shelf	1	25⅝ x 6½ x ½
birch bottom shelf	1	25⅛ x 10½ x ½
birch bottom board	1	26 x 11¼ x ⅝
birch side boards	2	33 x 12 x ⅝

(finished sizes, given in inches)

WORKING DRAWINGS AND DETAILS OF THE CYMA-CURVE HANGING SHELVES *measurements are given in inches*

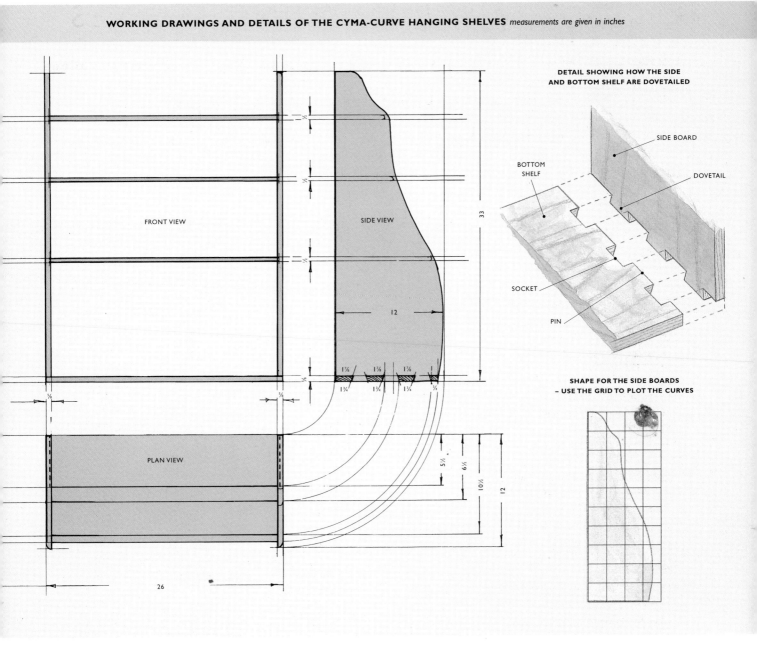

DETAIL SHOWING HOW THE SIDE
AND BOTTOM SHELF ARE DOVETAILED

SIDE BOARD

BOTTOM
SHELF

DOVETAIL

SOCKET

PIN

SHAPE FOR THE SIDE BOARDS
– USE THE GRID TO PLOT THE CURVES

FRONT VIEW

SIDE VIEW

PLAN VIEW

The New England woodworkers were masters of the curve. If you gave them a series of points – as expressed by the relationship between the width and the spacing of the four shelves shown in this project – they would have been able to draw out countless cyma curves.

Considering the design

This project has all the features of the classic wall-hung shelf. The shelves are graded in depth with the smallest being at the top. The profile of the side board flows in a smooth curve that uses the wood to best advantage and relates to the front of the shelves, and the bottom board or shelf is dovetailed into the side boards. The only detail that separates this shelf from its eighteenth-century New England cousins is the fact that it's made of European birch rather than American cherry or pine.

Preparing the wood

Take your six chosen boards – three shelves, a bottom board and two side boards – and check them over to make sure that they are free from knots, splits, and stains. As this is a relatively small piece, do your best to obtain boards that show good color and grain characteristics. Plane the wood to thickness, square up the edges, and label the best face sides and edges in pencil.

Laying out the design

Take the sheet of tracing paper and lay out the overall size of the side board at 33 in long and 12 in wide. Draw in the position and width of the shelves, and use the front-of-shelf points to establish the shape of the cyma-curve profile. When you are happy with the curve, thicken up the line with a soft pencil, and pencil press-transfer the line through to one of the two side boards (step 2).

Fretting the curve

The mistake that most people make with a project of this character is that they transfer the traced image through to both side boards, with the result that the two profiles come out slightly different. The best way is to fret out one cyma-curve board, and then to use the board as a template to cut out the second profile (step 3). Working in this way, the small variations that will inevitably occur will be transferred to the second board – the end result being that both boards will be identical.

Making the dovetails

Having cut the bottom board to size, set the gauge to ⅝ in, and run a line around both ends of the board. Mark out the pins with a bevel and square, and clear the waste with the coping saw and chisel.

Gauge a line around the bottom of the two side boards and use the cut pins to set out the shape of the tails. Clear the waste with the backsaw and the coping saw, and then use the chisel to pare the sockets to a good fit (step 4).

Making the shelves

Take the three shelves, all planed and sized, and use the hollow plane to shape the nosing. Secure the board in the vise and adjust the plane to make the finest skimming cut. Set the plane at a canted angle to the board, and start by shaving off the sharp angles (step 5). Continue in this way until the cross-section shape of the nosing fits the shape of the blade.

Making the housings

Take the side boards with the stopped dados clearly set out, and drill flat-bottomed holes at the stopped end of the dados. Sink the holes to the depth of 5⁄16 in. Use the marking knife and chisel to make angled tracks for the saw, and then run parallel saw cuts into the flat-bottomed hole. Gradually pare the waste down to the bottom of the saw cuts, and use the gouge to trim the stopped end of the dado to fit the profiled front edges of the shelves (step 6).

Assembly

Inspect all the component parts to make sure that you have not made any mistakes, then have a dry run assembly. Knock the dovetail joints together, and slide in the three shelf boards from the back of the unit so that the round edge profiles butt perfectly into the closed ends of the dados. You might need to use the gouge to trim the ends of the housings to a closer fit.

Finishing

When you are satisfied with the shelf, carefully disassemble the shelf unit and rub down all the surfaces to a smooth finish. Glue the shelf back together, and clamp up. Give 'all the surfaces a thin coat of Danish oil, burnish all surfaces with beeswax, and screw the two brass hanging plates in position on the back edges of the side boards (step 7).

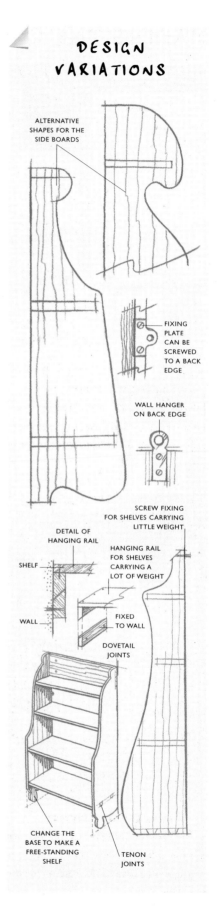

DESIGN VARIATIONS

ALTERNATIVE SHAPES FOR THE SIDE BOARDS

FIXING PLATE CAN BE SCREWED TO A BACK EDGE

WALL HANGER ON BACK EDGE

SCREW FIXING FOR SHELVES CARRYING LITTLE WEIGHT

DETAIL OF HANGING RAIL

HANGING RAIL FOR SHELVES CARRYING A LOT OF WEIGHT

SHELF

WALL

FIXED TO WALL

DOVETAIL JOINTS

CHANGE THE BASE TO MAKE A FREE-STANDING SHELF

TENON JOINTS

MAKING THE CYMA-CURVE HANGING SHELVES

1 Setting out the design
Draw up the side view of the shelves on tracing paper, and use the resulting reference points to map out the shape of the side board.

2 Transferring the design
Establish the precise shape of the curve by fixing the tracing in place with tabs of masking tape, and pencil press-transferring the traced lines through.

3 Duplicating the curved shape
Clamp the fretted board on the workpiece and score a duplicate shape.

4 Making the dovetails
Use a bevel-edge chisel to pare down to the gauged guide line.

5 Planing the shelf nosings
Secure the workpiece in the vise and use the hollow plane to cut the shelf nosing profile. Use this procedure for the top three shelves.

6 Cutting the dados
Use the in-cannel gouge to trim the stopped ends of the dado to fit the leading edge of the shelf. Aim for a tight-fitting, clean joint.

7 Fitting the hanging plates
Set in the shape of the plate with a knife, and cut the recess with the chisel.

TROUBLESHOOTING

- If you can get to use a band saw, or perhaps a good-sized bow saw, you can clamp the two side boards together and fret the two profiles out all of a piece.

- An in-cannel or channel gouge is characterized by having the bevel on the inside face of the blade – it is designed for cutting concave curves.

9: STEPPED SHELVES ON WHEELS

An easy-to-move magazine shelf, a coffee table, a shelf for the TV, or perhaps a side table for the patio, this shelf is all things to all people. Made in birch plywood, with four beautiful, easy-swivel, ball-bearing castor wheels, this is the perfect piece of furniture for a contemporary setting.

TOOLS AND MATERIALS

- band saw or rip saw
- crosscut saw
- block plane and grooving plane
- brace with small-sized drill bits
- marking knife, square, rule, gauge, and pencil
- graded sandpaper
- Danish oil and beeswax polish
- brads, ½ in long and 16 screws, 1⅛ in long
- birch plywood and beech (see cutting list)

CUTTING LIST

part	quantity	L x W x T
top board	1	20 x 18 x ½
base board	1	36 x 20 x ½
large end board	1	20 x 11⅜ x ½
small end board	1	20 x 5¼ x ½
middle vertical board	1	20 x 11¼ x ½
middle horizontal (left)	1	20 x 17½ x ½
middle horizontal (right)	1	20 x 18 x ½

all of the above are from birch plywood

4 beech wheel blocks	1	14 x 3¼ x 1

(finished sizes, given in inches)

Considering the design

Look at the working drawings and details. The project is made from top-quality ½ in-thick multi-core or veneer-core birch plywood, with castor wheels screwed to beech blocks, and the various plywood boards are jointed by means of barefaced tongues and grooves, which are glued and pinned. As to the techniques, while we have used an old grooving plane to cut the tongues and grooves, you could just as well use a

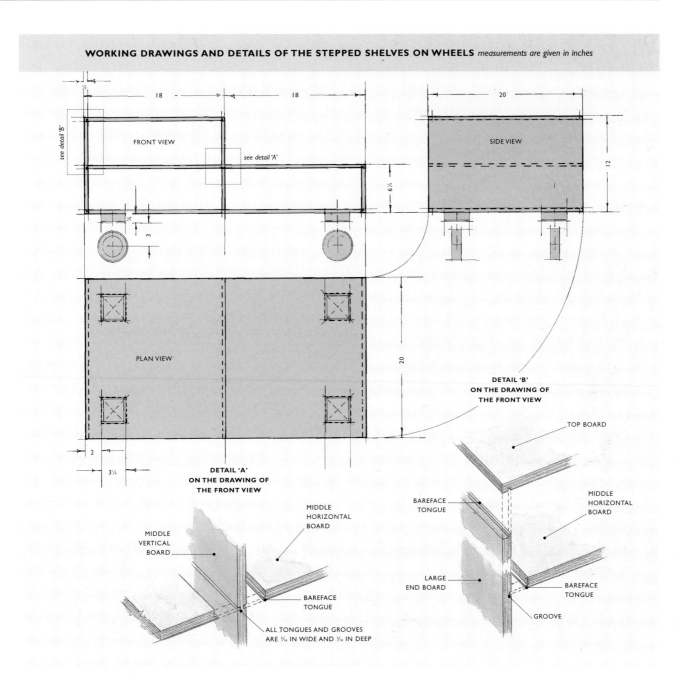

power router, a table saw, or even a mix of chisels, hand saws, and grooving planes. The choice is yours.

Preparing the wood

Take your seven sheets of plywood, all cut to size and squared at the edges – the top board, the base board, the two end boards, the middle vertical board, and the two middle horizontal boards – and check them over to make sure there are no awkwardly placed repairs, filled splits, delaminations and the like. If the problems are no more than superficial repairs, then arrange them so that they are on the inside or underside of the finished piece. Pencil-label every board so that you know where it fits in the scheme of things.

Setting out the joints

Study the working drawings and details, and see how, though the joints are all based on a tongue and a groove, the context of the various tongue-and-grooves not only requires slightly different laying out arrangements, but also different cutting procedures. All tongue-and-grooves are square in section – $\frac{3}{16}$ in wide and deep. When you have considered the options and have a clear understanding of how the various tongue-and-grooves need to be worked, lay them out with a rule, pencil, marking knife, and square (step 1).

Cutting the tongues

Having set out the tongues and scored them in with the marking knife, clamp the workpiece in the vise so that the edge to be worked is uppermost. Fit the grooving plane with the ³⁄₁₆ in blade and adjust it to make a light, skimming cut. Set the depth stop at ³⁄₁₆ in and the fence against the side of the blade. Now, starting at the end of the wood that is furthest away, apply a medium pressure with the left hand to keep the fence hard up against the face of the plywood, and apply only the lightest pressure with the right hand, and make the first cut. Repeat the procedure until the depth stop comes to rest (step 2).

Cutting the grooves

Note how the grooves occur in two situations – either ⁵⁄₁₆ in away from the edge of the plywood, as with the top board, or towards the middle of the plywood, as with the middle vertical board. The edge groove is no problem – you simply set up the plane in much the same way as already described and make the cut (step 3).

For the middle-of-board groove, remove the fence from the plane, clamp a strip of wood across the workpiece to act as a guide, score in the groove with a utility knife, and then make the cut (step 4). The knife cuts ensure that the grain is severed before the plane makes its cut, and so the groove has clean edges.

Making the wheel blocks

Take the piece of beech 14 in x 3¼ in x 1 in, and set out four 3¼ in lengths (allow for saw cut thicknesses). Run diagonals across the step-offs to fix the centers, then drill center holes to fit your chosen wheel fixings, and countersink holes for the screws. Use the block plane to run a delicate chamfer along both edges of the length of wood (step 5), then cut the wood into equal-sized square blocks and chamfer the sawn edges. Work from side to center so as not to split the grain (step 6).

Assembly and finishing

When you have cut all the tongues and grooves, then comes the tricky task of putting the project together. The best way is to set the base board down flat on the bench and have a trial run, making slight adjustments as you go. When you have achieved a good, square fit of all the parts, smear glue on mating faces, clamp up, and fix with ¾ in brads – four along each joint (step 7). Finally, bolt the wheels to the blocks, screw the blocks in place (step 8), rub down all surfaces and edges to a smooth finish, lay on a coat of Danish oil, and burnish with wax and a lint-free cloth.

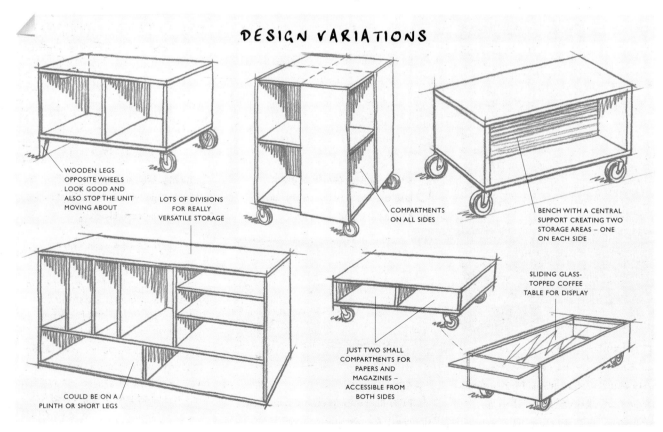

DESIGN VARIATIONS

WOODEN LEGS OPPOSITE WHEELS LOOK GOOD AND ALSO STOP THE UNIT MOVING ABOUT

LOTS OF DIVISIONS FOR REALLY VERSATILE STORAGE

COMPARTMENTS ON ALL SIDES

BENCH WITH A CENTRAL SUPPORT CREATING TWO STORAGE AREAS – ONE ON EACH SIDE

COULD BE ON A PLINTH OR SHORT LEGS

JUST TWO SMALL COMPARTMENTS FOR PAPERS AND MAGAZINES – ACCESSIBLE FROM BOTH SIDES

SLIDING GLASS-TOPPED COFFEE TABLE FOR DISPLAY

MAKING THE STEPPED SHELVES ON WHEELS

1 Scoring the joint guidelines
Set out the guidelines with a pencil, and score them in with a knife.

2 Cutting the tongues
Cut the tongues with the grooving plane. Hold the plane square to the side.

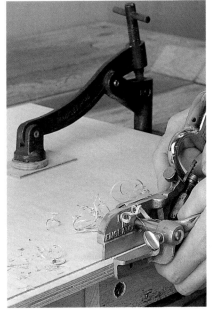

3 Planing the edge grooves
Cut the grooves with the grooving plane. Keep the fingers of the left hand underneath the board to ensure that the plane is square and upright.

4 Cutting the middle grooves
Set up a guide-strip fence parallel to the groove, clamp the guide so that the plane cutter is perfectly aligned, and make the cut.

5 Chamfering the block strip
Chamfer the edges of the wheel strip with the block plane. Tilt the plane slightly across the chamfer so as to make an oblique shearing cut.

6 Chamfering the end grain
Use the block plane to cut the chamfer on the end grain.

7 Assembling
Push-fit the tongues in the grooves, and check for overall squareness.

8 Fixing the wheel blocks
Screw the wheel blocks in place – four screws to each block.

TROUBLESHOOTING

- If you enjoy cutting tongue-and-grooves with a hand plane, you could search secondhand tool stores for an old Record 405 or a Stanley 45 combination plane.

- If you are at all unsure about cutting a groove with a plane, it is best to have several trial runs on scrap wood before you start the project.

10: SYSTEM SHELVES

Made in cherry and beech, with the two poles being either turned or found, and with the shelves being fixed with whittled pins or pegs, this shelving unit draws its inspiration from the refreshingly uncomplicated furniture that was made in Europe in the late 1950s.

TOOLS AND MATERIALS

- band saw, thicknesser and surface planer
- crosscut saw
- scroll saw (or coping saw)
- bench plane and block plane
- bench drill (or brace), forstner drill bit (1⅛ in diameter), drill bits ⅜ in and ¼ in in diameter
- square, rule, marking gauge, and pencil
- utility knife, Swedish sloyd knife, or small penknife
- no. 8 screws: 8 x countersunk, and 8 x round-headed with 8 washers
- cabinet scrape, and fine sandpaper
- Danish oil and beeswax polish
- cherry and beech (see cutting list)

CUTTING LIST

part	quantity	L x W x T
cherry back boards	2	47 x 3 x ¾
cherry shelves	4	15 x 15 x ¾
cherry pegs (cut from)	1	48 x 1 x 1
beech poles	2	49 x 1⅛ diam.

(finished sizes, given in inches)

The design is beautifully direct – just four shelves, two planks, and a couple of poles (which you can lathe-turn or buy ready-made), all held together with screws and pegs. If you are looking to make a unit that can be dismantled – a unit that is both easy to make and contemporary – then perhaps this is the one to choose.

Considering the design

Look at the working drawings. See how, with all the shelves, the outer screws fix the position of the shelf in relation to the back board, while the inner screws are fixed through slots that allow for slight movement. Consider the way that the whittled pegs are tapped in from the front of the shelves, with the head of the peg being a decorative feature.

Preparing the wood

Take your wood and check it over for possible problems. Decide how knots and marked differences in grain texture and color need to be placed.

Plane the wood true – all as described in the Tools and Techniques section – and spend time identifying and marking the best faces and edges. Cut the two boards and the four shelves to length, and use a block plane and a bench plane to tidy up the sawn end-grain edges.

Setting out the back boards

Take the two boards and use a rule, square, and pencil to mark the shelf positions. Starting from the foot of the board, set out step-offs alternately at 11 in and ¾ in (shelf thickness). Establish the position of the screw holes and use the square to run guidelines across the back of both boards.

Setting out the shelves

Take the shelves and label them so that you know where each is going. Decide how far back from the edges of the shelves the poles need to be set – this will depend on the diameter of your poles – and use a pencil and square to mark the center points for the holes. Establish the position of the peg holes by squaring lines from the pole centers (step 1).

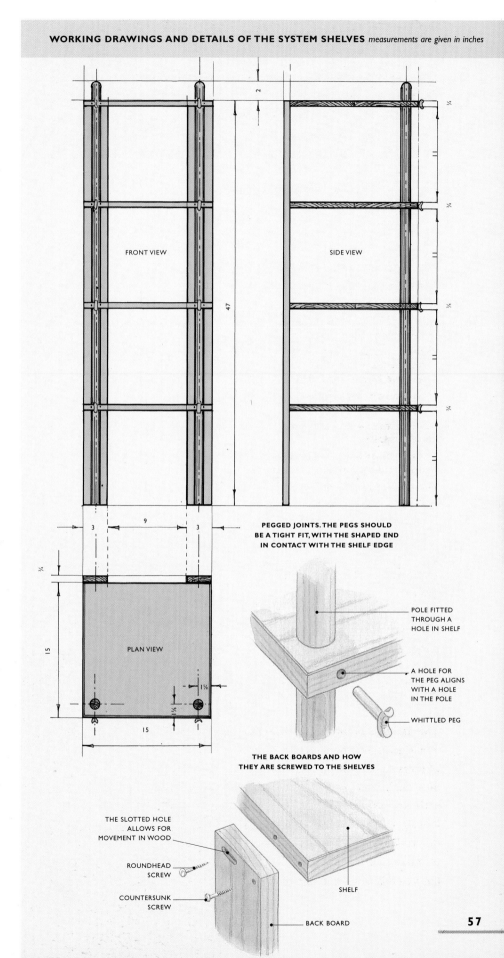

WORKING DRAWINGS AND DETAILS OF THE SYSTEM SHELVES *measurements are given in inches*

FRONT VIEW

SIDE VIEW

PLAN VIEW

PEGGED JOINTS. THE PEGS SHOULD BE A TIGHT FIT, WITH THE SHAPED END IN CONTACT WITH THE SHELF EDGE

POLE FITTED THROUGH A HOLE IN SHELF

A HOLE FOR THE PEG ALIGNS WITH A HOLE IN THE POLE

WHITTLED PEG

THE BACK BOARDS AND HOW THEY ARE SCREWED TO THE SHELVES

THE SLOTTED HOLE ALLOWS FOR MOVEMENT IN WOOD

ROUNDHEAD SCREW

COUNTERSUNK SCREW

SHELF

BACK BOARD

57

Cutting the pole and peg holes

Use a forstner drill bit and drill press for boring the pole holes through the shelves. Set a slab of waste board on the drill table, position the workpiece and clamp it in place. Drill carefully so as to avoid exit damage (step 2).

For the peg holes, fit a ¼ in bit in the brace and run the peg holes through from the front edge – so that the hole is targeted at the center of the pole.

Making the poles

When you have the poles – either turned or store-bought – decide on the design of the pole as it appears on the top shelf. There are many possible options. You could cut off the top of the pole flush with the shelf and make the end grain a feature, or you could go for a whittled finial that reflects the design of the pegs, and so on. We decided to have the pole standing up a full 2 in from the shelf, with the top smoothly rounded.

Cutting the screw holes

Take the two back boards and label them "left" and "right". Aim, with the top and bottom shelves, to have the screw hole about ¾ in in from the outside edge, and make the slot ¾ in long and set ¾ in in from the inside edge (step 3). One way of making the slot is to drill two holes about ¾ in apart and then use a coping saw to clear the waste, and a fold of sandpaper to tidy up (step 4).

Whittling the pegs

Take the wood that you have chosen for the pegs and cut it into eight equal lengths. Mark off each piece at a point about 1 in along from one end. Grasp the workpiece by what will become the shaped end, and whittle the shank

so that it's a tight, easy push-fit in the peg hole.

When you have skimmed the shank of the peg down to size, then comes the task of whittling the shaped end. We have gone for a bone-like form, but you could design yours differently. Work with a tight, apple-paring stroke – all the while making sure that you cut from high to low wood, and avoid cutting directly into end grain. Continue carving until you have what you consider is a good shape (step 5).

Fitting

When you have finished the shelves, boards, and pegs, it is time to have a dry run fitting. Set the shelves in order on the floor – so that they are standing on the front edge – and then bridge them with the two back boards and drive in the screws (step 6). Having eased the two poles through the four shelves – and being very

careful that you don't put undue pressure on the screws – stand the unit upright and use a rule and level to establish the precise position of the shelves. Lastly, when you are absolutely sure that all is correct, run the peg holes through the thickness of the pole and beyond, and push the pegs into place (steps 7 and 8).

Finishing

Before you apply the finish, check that the shelves are stable and that the joints are working. Disassemble the shelf unit, and use the scraper and sandpaper to bring all surfaces to a smooth finish. Pay particular attention to the uppermost surface of the shelves, the top of the poles, and the pegs. Give all surfaces a thin coat of Danish oil and allow them to dry. Burnish all the surfaces with the beeswax polish, re-assemble, and the shelves are ready for use.

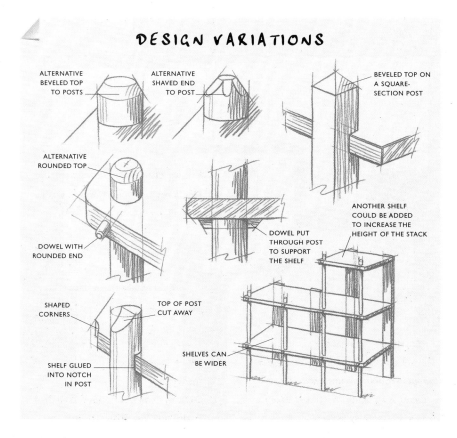

DESIGN VARIATIONS

ALTERNATIVE BEVELED TOP TO POSTS

ALTERNATIVE SHAVED END TO POST

BEVELED TOP ON A SQUARE-SECTION POST

ALTERNATIVE ROUNDED TOP

DOWEL WITH ROUNDED END

DOWEL PUT THROUGH POST TO SUPPORT THE SHELF

ANOTHER SHELF COULD BE ADDED TO INCREASE THE HEIGHT OF THE STACK

SHAPED CORNERS

TOP OF POST CUT AWAY

SHELF GLUED INTO NOTCH IN POST

SHELVES CAN BE WIDER

MAKING THE SYSTEM SHELVES

1 Positioning the holes
Use a square and dividers to establish the precise position for the hole. Choose a drill bit diameter the same as the pole – so that the pole is a neat push-fit.

2 Drilling the shelf holes
Set the shelf slab on a piece of waste, clamp the assembly to the drill-press table – so that the bit is accurately aligned – and run the hole through.

3 Measuring the fixing holes
Use a rule and dividers to set out the position of the screw hole and slot.

4 Cutting the screw slot
Pass the blade through the pilot hole, and cut out the slot.

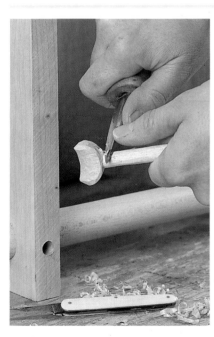

5 Trimming the pegs
Tidy up the whittling by running a stop-cut around the underside of the head and shaving up the shank. Work with a tight, thumb-braced action.

6 Fixing the back boards
Use a roundhead screw in a slot to fix the back boards to the shelves.

7 Assembly
Slide the poles through the shelves and make sure the structure is square.

8 Drilling the peg holes
Clamp the arrangement securely and run the peg holes through the pole.

TROUBLESHOOTING

- If the unit is a bit shaky, then the chances are that the poles are a sloppy, loose fit through the shelves.
- Be careful when you are setting out the shelves, that you don't have the pole holes positioned too near the side edges – i.e. the end-grain edges.

11: PLATE DISPLAY SHELVES

The notion of a plate display shelf goes way back to the Elizabethans, the New England settlers, the Shakers, the Pennsylvania Germans, Dutch, French, Spanish... When plates and dishes were readily available, these communities soon developed display shelves to put them on.

TOOLS AND MATERIALS

- rip saw, band saw, or pre-milled lumber
- crosscut saw
- bench hook
- bench drill with forstner drill bits ¼ in and ¾ in in diameter
- five planes: bench, block, rabbet, hand router, and small chisel-nose shoulder plane
- selection of bevel-edge paring chisels
- mortise gauge
- square, compass, rule, and pencil
- marking knife and straight edge
- pair of bar clamps with a reach greater than the width of the finished unit
- small brad hammer
- PVA glue and 1¼ in pins
- graded sandpaper
- Danish oil and beeswax polish
- 8 x rose-headed nails, 1 in long
- American red oak (see cutting list)

CUTTING LIST

part	quantity	L x W x T
oak side boards	2	28 x 5 x ¾
oak top board	1	49 x 5¾ x ⅞
oak shelves	3	44¼ x 5 x ¾
oak tongue-and-groove back boards to make up a total area of:	1	44⅛ x 28½ x ⅝
oak rails	4	44⅛ x 1 x ½

(finished sizes, given in inches)

WORKING DRAWINGS AND DETAIL OF THE PLATE DISPLAY SHELVES *measurements are given in inches*

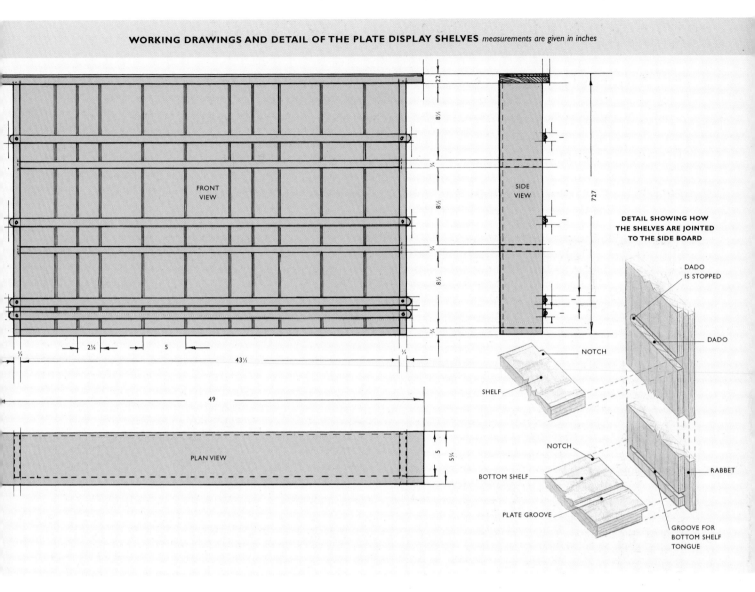

FRONT VIEW

SIDE VIEW

DETAIL SHOWING HOW THE SHELVES ARE JOINTED TO THE SIDE BOARD

DADO IS STOPPED

DADO

NOTCH

SHELF

NOTCH

BOTTOM SHELF

PLATE GROOVE

RABBET

GROOVE FOR BOTTOM SHELF TONGUE

PLAN VIEW

Considering the design

Study the working drawings, and see how this shelf has all the classic features: a top board with a generous overhang, shelves with furrows, and thin battens to act as a gallery. Note that the whole piece is made from American red oak.

Preparing the wood

Spread out your chosen wood on the bench and check it over for problems. Reject end splits and dead knots. Arrange the grain for best effect, and generally make decisions as to what goes where and how. Plane the wood to thickness and width, and mark face sides and edges. Label each board so that you know how it is placed.

Laying out the side boards

Take the two side boards, and use the measure, straightedge, and square to lay out the total length, the back edge rabbet, the stopped dados at ¾ in wide for the two middle shelves, and the bottom groove at ¼ in wide – at a position about ½ in up from the bottom end. Set out the stopped ends of the dados with circles and center points to suit the drill bit diameters (step 1).

Laying out the top and bottom boards

Lay out the top board to length at 49 in, and draw in the position of the side board dados at ¾ in wide – at a point 2 in along from the ends. Now take the bottom board, and lay out the thickness and width of the end rabbet tongues.

Cutting the dados and rabbets

Check that the dados are all accurately set out – the correct position, length, and width – and use the appropriate size drill bit to sink the stopped ends into a depth of ³/₁₆ in. The procedure for cutting stopped dados is as follows. Score in the width of the dados with a knife and square. Run a chisel at an angle to the waste side of the scored line – so as to pare a furrow that cants into the line – and then take repeated light cuts with the router towards the stopped end. Continue until the whole groove is down to the depth of the drilled hole (step 2).

To cut the stopped rabbet along the back edge of the top board, set the gauge to ⅝ in, and run it along both face and back edge. Secure the board down flat on the bench. Take the rabbet plane, clamp a batten fence to the side of the line, and run the plane from one end through to the other. When the rabbet is down to the point where the nose of the plane comes to a halt against the stopped end, then change over to using the chisel plane to complete the cut (step 3). Use a narrow bevel-edge chisel to clean up the corners and angles (step 4).

Cutting the plate grooves

Take the three boards – the two middle shelves and the bottom shelf – and draw in the position of the leading edge of the plate groove at about 2½ in from the front edge of the shelf. Score in the line with a knife to make a stop-cut, and use a chisel to pare into the cut so as to make a slightly angled track.

Adjust the rabbet plane to make a light cut, set it at an angle in the track, and make repeated cuts until you have a sloping level that runs down into the bottom of your initial stop-cut (step 5). Finally, set the plane on its side in the groove and tidy up the other face that goes to make the "V" shape.

Assembly

When you have completed all the joints and cuts that go to make up the project – the dados, rabbets, plate grooves, the notched ends to the shelves, and all the rest – clean the work surface, and set the boards together so that the back edges are uppermost. Slide the top ends of the side boards into the dados on the underside of the top board; ease the shelves into the side board dados, and adjust for a good fit.

When you are fitting the bottom shelf into the narrow dado, be very careful that you don't break off the relatively fragile short grain that occurs between the side of the housing and the bottom end of the board (step 6). Trim and adjust the structure until it is square. Cut the tongue-and-groove boards to length so that they are neatly contained by

the rabbet on the side board, and the back edge of the bottom shelf (step 7). Have the decorative face of the boards on view.

Finishing

When you have adjusted the components so that they are a good fit, run chamfers on the edge of the top board, and use the graded sandpapers to rub down all the surfaces to a smooth finish. Pencil-label the parts, and then disassemble the whole piece. Glue and clamp the side boards to the top board and the bottom shelf. Clamp and pin the back boards to the shelves and top board. When the glue is set, remove the clamps, drill pilot holes through the ends of the rails, and fix them to the side boards with the rose-headed nails (step 8). Finally, lay on a coat of Danish oil, let it dry, and burnish with beeswax.

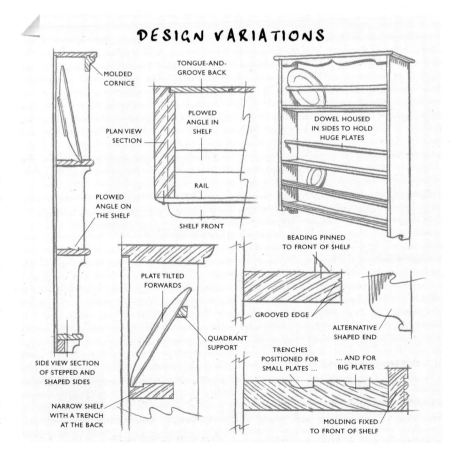

DESIGN VARIATIONS

MOLDED CORNICE

TONGUE-AND-GROOVE BACK

PLAN VIEW SECTION

PLOWED ANGLE IN SHELF

PLOWED ANGLE ON THE SHELF

RAIL

SHELF FRONT

DOWEL HOUSED IN SIDES TO HOLD HUGE PLATES

SIDE VIEW SECTION OF STEPPED AND SHAPED SIDES

NARROW SHELF WITH A TRENCH AT THE BACK

PLATE TILTED FORWARDS

QUADRANT SUPPORT

BEADING PINNED TO FRONT OF SHELF

GROOVED EDGE

ALTERNATIVE SHAPED END

TRENCHES POSITIONED FOR SMALL PLATES ...

... AND FOR BIG PLATES

MOLDING FIXED TO FRONT OF SHELF

MAKING THE PLATE DISPLAY SHELVES

Setting out the dados
Use a compass to establish the position of the drilled holes. Choose a forstner drill bit to match up with the width of the dados.

2 Routing the dado
Set the router gauge to the depth of the dado, and clear the waste.

3 Completing the rabbet
Use the chisel plane to cut the stopped end of the rabbet.

4 Paring the dado
Finish cutting the dado at the bottom of the sides with the chisel. Be careful that you don't split off the fragile short grain.

5 Cutting the plate grooves
Cut the plate grooves with the rabbet plane held at an angle. Maintain the angle by tucking your fingertips between the sole and the workpiece.

6 Assembling
Fit the bottom shelf into the end board rabbet, and trim to fit.

7 Fitting the back boards
Cut the tongue-and-groove back boards to length and set them in place.

8 Fixing the rails
Run pilot holes through the rails and fix them with the rose-headed nails.

TROUBLESHOOTING

- If you can't get a hand router plane to cut the dados, then you could use a power router, or even a mix of a saw and chisel.

- At the clamping stage, be very careful that you don't over-tighten the clamps and break off the delicate wood at the end of the side boards.

12: FRENCH PROVINCIAL SHELF

This pretty little shelf has many of the features that characterize early twentieth-century French provincial furniture. Romantic, naïve, a country-cousin interpretation of a more sophisticated form, this is the perfect shelf for a cottage kitchen.

TOOLS AND MATERIALS

- band saw or rip saw, or pre-milled lumber
- crosscut saw and small backsaw
- power scroll saw (or coping saw)
- bench plane and block plane
- bench drill (or brace)
- three forstner drill bits: a large-diameter 1¼ in bit, and two smaller bits at 3/16 in and ⅜ in
- square, bevel square, dividers or compasses, rule, and pencil
- selection of bevel-edge chisels
- power sander and graded sandpaper
- watercolor paint (color to suit)
- Danish oil
- selection of screws, small dowels, and cup hooks
- PVA glue
- brads, 1 in long
- pine (see cutting list)

CUTTING LIST

part	quantity	L x W x T
top shelf	1	28½ x 9 x ¾
bottom shelf	1	26 x 6 x ¾
top horizontal batten	1	29½ x 1⅝ x ¾
second horizontal batten	1	26 x 3¼ x ¾
other horizontal battens	2	29½ x 3¼ x ¾
vertical battens	2	49¼ x 67 x ⅞
brackets	4	¾ in-thick offcuts
bottom shelf edge strip	1	26 x ⅝ x ⅝

All of the above are in pine

(finished sizes, given in inches)

WORKING DRAWINGS AND DETAILS OF THE FRENCH PROVINCIAL SHELF *measurements are given in inches*

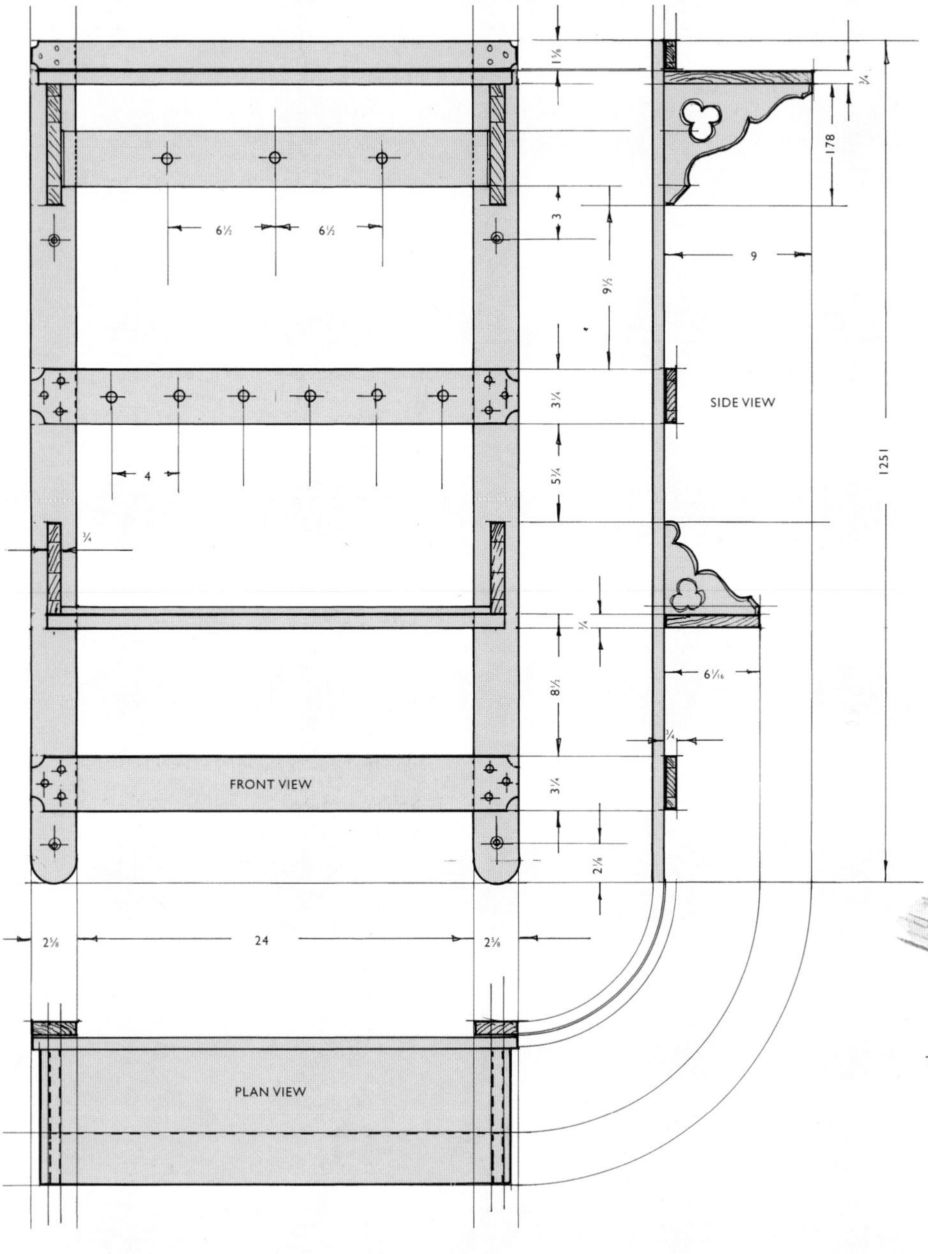

SIDE VIEW

FRONT VIEW

PLAN VIEW

SHAPES FOR BRACKETS

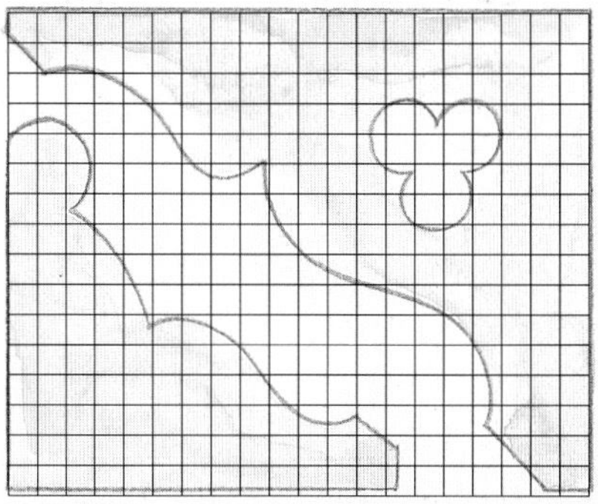

DETAIL OF TOP CORNER OF SHELVES

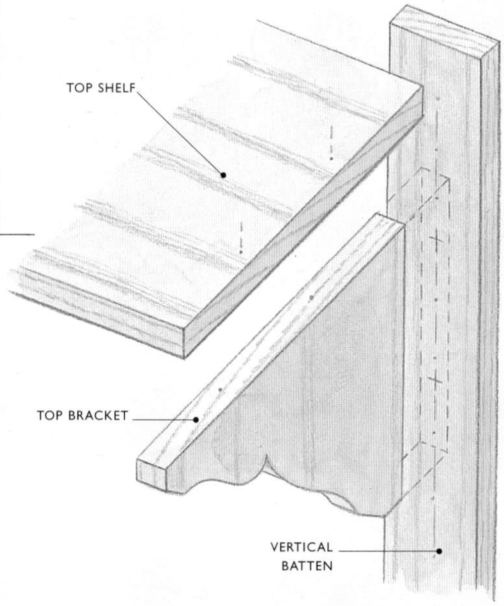

TOP SHELF

TOP BRACKET

VERTICAL
BATTEN

This is a delightfully easy project to make: no expensive woods or complex joinery, it is simply sawn and drilled, screwed, bradded, and pegged together, and then color-washed. If you are looking for a shelf that speaks of quarry tiles, earthenware jugs, onion soup, and brown bread dipped in olive oil, then this is the one.

Considering the design
Study the working drawings and see how the shelf is made up from prepared lengths of pine, with drilled and fretted brackets. The whole thing is put together with screws, nails, and dowels. The "carved" trefoils are beautifully direct – just a bit of compass work and three drilled holes. As for

the brass hooks, while we chose to have three large hooks for milk jugs, and six hooks for teacups, you can of course go for an arrangement that suits your needs. The finish is wonderfully easy to achieve – all you do is lay on a thin watercolor wash (choose a color to match your decor) and rub through to reveal the grain.

Preparing the wood

Label all the lengths so that you know how they relate to one another. Position the top, middle, and bottom battens across the two verticals, square them to length, and fix the position of the shelf brackets. Draw out the shape of the brackets, and set out the groundwork for the trefoil decoration (step 1).

Making the brackets and battens

Having set out the shape of the four brackets, move to the scroll saw – or you might be using a hand coping saw or even a small bow saw – and start fretting out the profiles. It is best to run straight cuts through to the sharp angles, and then fret out the individual curves as separate pieces (step 2). When you have double-checked that the guide lines for the trefoils are correctly placed, and have maybe had a trial drilling on some scrap wood,

move to the drill and bore out the holes that go to make up the design. Note how the decorative trefoil holes in the top bracket run right through the thickness of the wood (step 3), while in the bottom bracket the holes only run halfway through the thickness (step 4). Use the scroll saw to shape the ends of the battens.

Assembly

Sand all thirteen component parts to a smooth finish – the two verticals, the four brackets, the six horizontals and the edge strip. Set down the two verticals on the bench, screw-fix the cross-battens at top and bottom – with single screws at center – and dowel the brackets in place (step 5). Check for squareness and stabilize the whole structure by butting the shelves hard up against both the vertical battens and the brackets, and fix with screws (step 6). Screw the hook boards in position, (step 7), and decide

on how you want the various hooks to be placed. When you are pleased with the overall arrangement, remove the temporary holding screws one at a time, and fix permanently with screws and plugs. Pare the tops off the dowel plugs with a chisel (step 8), and rub them down to a flush finish. Glue and pin the edge strip in place.

Finishing

Remove the screw hooks, vacuum up the dust, and move to a dust-free area. Mix your chosen color with water (so that you have a thin wash) and have a try-out on a piece of scrap wood, and then lay on repeated coats of wash until you have what you consider is a good density of color. Wait until the paint is dry, then rub down with the fine-grade sandpaper until all surfaces are smooth to the touch, and you have revealed the grain in selected areas. Finally, lay on a thin coat of Danish oil.

DESIGN VARIATIONS

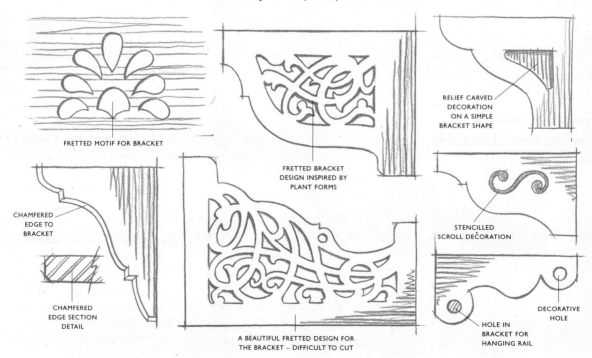

FRETTED MOTIF FOR BRACKET

CHAMFERED EDGE TO BRACKET

CHAMFERED EDGE SECTION DETAIL

FRETTED BRACKET DESIGN INSPIRED BY PLANT FORMS

A BEAUTIFUL FRETTED DESIGN FOR THE BRACKET – DIFFICULT TO CUT

RELIEF CARVED DECORATION ON A SIMPLE BRACKET SHAPE

STENCILLED SCROLL DECORATION

HOLE IN BRACKET FOR HANGING RAIL

DECORATIVE HOLE

MAKING THE FRENCH PROVINCIAL SHELF

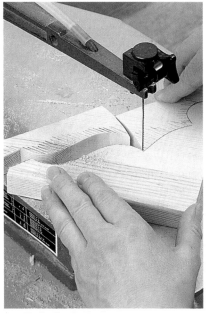

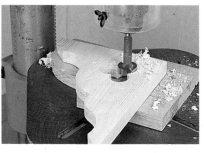

3 Drilling the pierced trefoil
Set the bracket on the waste and drill through the thickness of the wood.

4 Drilling the blind trefoil
Run the blind holes about halfway through the thickness of the wood.

1 Drawing out the brackets
Use the bevel square and compass to set out the bracket shape and trefoil motif. Refer to the gridded design details on page 65.

2 Cutting the brackets
Cut out the brackets with the scroll saw. Run a straight cut into the sharp angle, and then finish cutting the curves from the opposite direction.

5 Fixing the brackets
Spread glue in the holes and locate the bracket on the dowels.

6 Dry assembling
Stabilize the structure by butting the horizontals against the brackets.

7 Setting out the hook board
Set the hook board in place across the frame and position the six hooks so that they are evenly distributed along the length of the board.

8 Paring the dowel plugs
Hold the bevel-edge chisel at a low angle and pare the glued plugs flush.

TROUBLESHOOTING

- If you like the overall design but can't get to use a large-diameter drill bit, you could replace the drilled trefoil with a stencil-painted motif.

- The initial fixing with the single screws at the center allows the frame to be squared true prior to fixing with the other screws.

13: AMERICAN "CRAFTSMAN" BOOKCASE

Like the bookcase on page 40, this beautifully austere bookcase also pays homage to the "craftsman" style of furniture made in America between 1884 and 1915, by Gustav Stickley and others. We have picked up on the characteristic design details – the shape of the handle-like feature, and the profile of the plinth.

TOOLS AND MATERIALS

- band saw or rip saw, or pre-milled lumber
- crosscut saw and small backsaw
- good-size coping saw (or bow saw)
- three planes: bench, block, and shoulder or small rabbet
- hand router (or power router)
- small in-curve spokeshave
- brace with good-size bit
- square, compass, rule, and pencil
- marking knife
- single-pin gauge and mortise gauge
- selection of chisels, to include a mortise or general bevel of ⅜ in, and a wide one of about 1 in
- power sander and graded sandpaper
- PVA glue
- Danish oil and beeswax polish
- American oak (see cutting list)

CUTTING LIST

part	quantity	L x W x T
oak side boards	2	56½ x 13 x ¾
oak shelves	4	23½ x 13 x ¾
oak plinth boards	2	22¾ x 5 x ¾

(finished sizes, given in inches)

The wonderful thing about the American "craftsman" style is the way that it draws its inspiration in turn from William Morris and the English Arts and Crafts Movement.

Considering the design

Look at the working drawings and notes. This is a relatively uncomplicated piece, with the horizontal members being housed in the vertical side boards, and with the top and bottom shelves being through-tenoned to pull the whole structure together. Be mindful that the mere fact that the design is so uncomplicated means that its success hinges on the details being worked with extreme care. Or to put it another way, the design is so direct and honest that mistakes can't be hidden – all the details and joints are in full view.

Preparing the wood

Take your wood and check it over for problems – avoid splits and loose knots. If there is any sign of the wood splitting, then either do your best to make sure that the split occurs at what will be the foot of the side board, or go for another piece of wood. Plane the wood true and mark the best faces and edges. Cut the eight components to length – the four shelves, the two side boards, and the two plinth boards.

Setting out the design details

Having used the square to set out the position of the eight mortises, use the compass to set out the handle-like details at the top end of the two side boards (step 1). Draw the half-circle with the compass, the small radius curves by eye, the foot profile with the compass set at a radius of 2 in, and the plinth profile with tracing paper.

Setting out the joints

Look the four boards over, and select the best two lengths for the top and bottom shelves. Use the square and gauge to mark out the tenons at

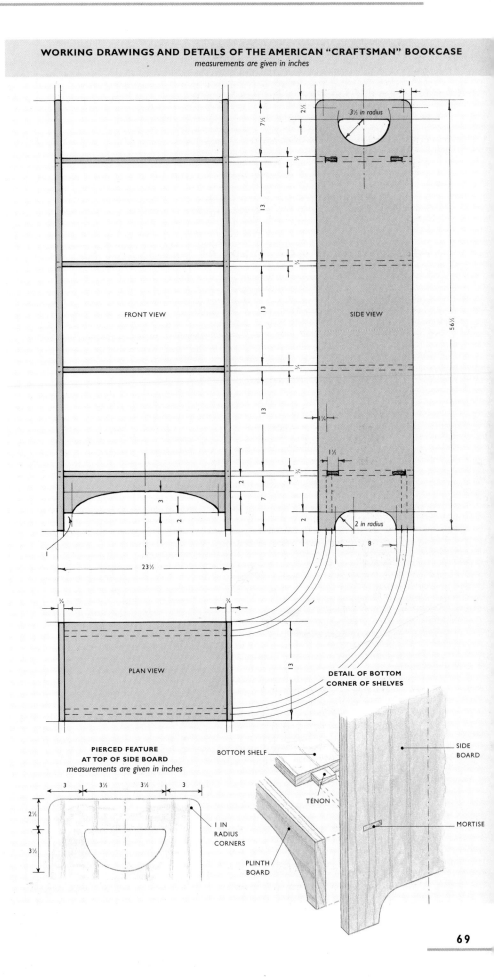

WORKING DRAWINGS AND DETAILS OF THE AMERICAN "CRAFTSMAN" BOOKCASE
measurements are given in inches

FRONT VIEW

SIDE VIEW

3½ in radius

2 in radius

PLAN VIEW

DETAIL OF BOTTOM CORNER OF SHELVES

PIERCED FEATURE AT TOP OF SIDE BOARD
measurements are given in inches

1 IN RADIUS CORNERS

BOTTOM SHELF

TENON

SIDE BOARD

MORTISE

PLINTH BOARD

1½ in wide and ⅜ in thick – so that the shoulders are about ³⁄₁₆ in wide. Have the tenons set about 1¼ in in from what will be the back and front edges of the shelf (step 3). Set out the corresponding mortises in the two side boards, and the dados for the plinth boards. Shade the waste.

Cutting the joints

Use the bow or coping saw to swiftly fret out the shape of the foot profile. Cut out the mortises and the plinth dados. Chop in with the heavy mortise chisel. Clear out the resultant chips of waste with a light chisel, and then pare the sides clean with a bevel-edge chisel (step 4). If you have doubts about size and fit, then it is best to err towards cutting too small and make adjustments later.

Cutting the dados

The shelf dados are best cut with a hand router. Set out the dado with a knife and square, set in the sides of the dado with a backsaw, and clear the waste with the router (step 5). The trick here is to make sure that the initial saw cuts are parallel and to the waste side of the drawn line.

Cutting the plinth boards

Cut the two plinth boards to length, and cut the dado and stopped joints. When you have achieved what you consider is a good fit, it is then time to work the feature curve. While there are many ways forward – you might use a band saw, a coping saw, or even a hand-held jig saw – we opted to use a bow saw and spokeshave. Run the saw cuts down from end to center – so that the cut edge is square to the face of the wood. Set the plinth in the vise at a comfortable height and use the spokeshave to skim the sawn edge

to a smooth finish. Work from end to center to avoid cutting directly into end grain (step 6).

Fretting the pierced feature

Drill a pilot hole through the window of waste and set the board in the vise so that the working area is at a comfortable height. Take the bow saw, unhitch the blade, pass one end of the blade through the pilot hole, re-hitch and re-tension, and then set to work fretting out the shape. All the while, make sure that the blade is held square to the face of the wood, and the line of cut is a little to the waste side of the drawn line. Work at an even pace so as to minimize grain breakout on the push stroke.

Assembly

When you have finished the component parts – all cut and partially rubbed down – set them out and

generally check them over for fit and finish. Set one side board down flat on the workbench, and set the two plinth boards in place in the dados. Slide the bottom shelf into position and ease the two tenons home (step 8). Finally, fit the top shelf, set the other side board in place, slide the other two shelves home, and clench up.

Finishing

When you are completely satisfied with the way the components come together, disassemble the whole piece, and use the graded sandpapers to rub down to a smooth finish. Aim for a crisp, round-edge finish on the top edges and around the pierced holes. Glue and clamp up, and leave overnight. Lastly, clean up the dust, give all the surfaces a thin coat of Danish oil, burnish the complete unit with wax, and… you have a perfect Stickley-inspired bookcase.

DESIGN VARIATIONS

REVERSE OF BASE PROFILE

PIERCED DETAIL

TROUGH SHAPE FOR BOOKS

TIGHTLY SPACED SHELVES FOR MAGAZINES AND PAPERWORK

WEDGED TENONS

TUSKED TENONS

ROUNDED CORNERS

SLAB TOP

GOUGE-EDGE PATTERN

TAPERED SIDES

TAPERED SHAPE BOTH WAYS

SHELF EXTENDS THROUGH SIDES

MAKING THE AMERICAN "CRAFTSMAN" BOOKCASE

1 Setting out the side board detail
Use a compass, dividers, and square to set out the side board feature.

2 Drawing the feet
Draw out the foot radius at 2 in – two quarter-circles set 8 in apart.

3 Marking the shelf tenons
Use the square to set out the tenons – 1½ in wide and ⅜ in thick.

4 Chopping the side mortises
Chop in with the mortise chisel and clean up with the bevel-edge chisel.

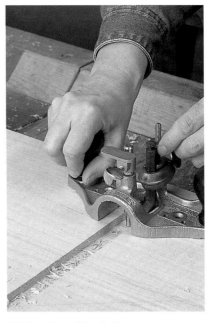

5 Routing the dados
Set the depth gauge to the full depth of the dado, and make repeated passes with the router until the required depth is achieved.

6 Trimming the plinth board
Use the spokeshave to shape and smooth the plinth board. Work from end to center – so that you are always cutting with the direction of the grain.

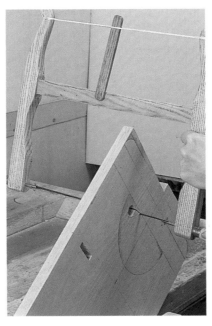

7 Fretting the pierced feature
Cut the handle-like details at the top of the side boards with the bow saw. Repeatedly adjust the frame of the saw so that it clears the wood.

8 Assembling
Put the parts together, being careful not to bruise the wood.

TROUBLESHOOTING

- If you want to speed up the action, you could use a band saw for cutting the plinth board.

- If you want to stay very close to the Stickley tradition, you could use thicker oak and stain it to a deep green-bronze finish.

14: HERB-DRYING SHELF

This simple country-kitchen shelf draws its inspiration from the folk art woodwork that has been made by the Amish, Mennonite, and other German-speaking communities in Pennsylvania since the seventeenth century. It is made from pine and designed for drying and storing herbs.

TOOLS AND MATERIALS

- band saw and planer-thicknesser
- small backsaw and coping saw
- block plane and shoulder plane
- bench drill (or brace), forstner drill bit 2 in in diameter, and a twist bit ¼ in in diameter
- square, rule, dividers, and pencil
- marking gauge and mortise gauge
- mortise chisels: ⅜ in and 1½ in
- 8 x screws, 1¼ in long
- fine sandpaper
- Danish oil and beeswax polish
- pine (see cutting list)

CUTTING LIST

part	quantity	L x W x T
pine shelf battens	4	48 x 1¼ x ⅞
pine brackets	2	50 x 2½ x ⅞
pine heart board	1	38 x 4½ x ½

(finished sizes, given in inches)

The Pennsylvanian German-speaking immigrants used the heart motif on just about everything, from embroidery, metalwork, woodcarving, and fracturs, through to biscuit cutters, pottery, and of course furniture.

If you want to make a good, solid, low-cost, functional shelf – a shelf that speaks of kitchen-hearth comforts, the old world, and feelings of family – or you just want to make a token of love for your nearest and dearest, then this has got to be the one.

Considering the design

Look at the working drawings and notes. See how the relatively basic structure – just two archetypal brackets linked by a board and a number of battens – is lifted above the ordinary by the inclusion of paired mortise and tenon joints at the back of the brackets, and the beautiful pierced heart motif placed at the center. This shelf has a lot to recommend it – it uses readily available low-cost lumber, it's quick and simple to make, it's eminently functional, and it's decorative.

Preparing the wood

Take your chosen wood and check it over for potential problems – avoid splits and loose knots. If there are a few characteristic knots, make sure that they are well clear of the mortise and tenon joints and the pierced heart. Plane the wood true and mark the best faces and edges. Use the tool

of your choice to cut radius curves on the top edges of the battens. We used an old Stanley 45 combination plane for this procedure, but you could just as well use a router, or a spokeshave, or even a mix of a block plane and a sanding block. Cut the eleven components to length – the four battens that go to make the shelf, the heart board, and the six pieces that go to make the two brackets. Plane the ends of the battens to a good finish.

Piercing the heart

Having studied the working drawings, take the heart board and square a center line halfway along its length. Use a pencil, rule, square, and dividers to set out the shape of the heart

(step 1). Spike the center points of the two circles. Set the large forstner bit in the drill press and bore out the two holes that make the cheeks of the heart. Take it slowly so that the holes are clean cut (step 2). Set the board in the vise, and use the coping saw to fret out the lower part of the heart shape. Lastly, use a fold of sandpaper to rub down the sawn edges to a smooth, slightly round-edge finish.

Cutting the mortise and tenons

Take the wood that you have chosen for the brackets and cut it down to size – so that you have two uprights, two bearers, and two brace pieces. Use a rule, square, and mortise gauge

WORKING DRAWINGS AND DETAILS OF THE HERB-DRYING SHELF *measurements are given in inches*

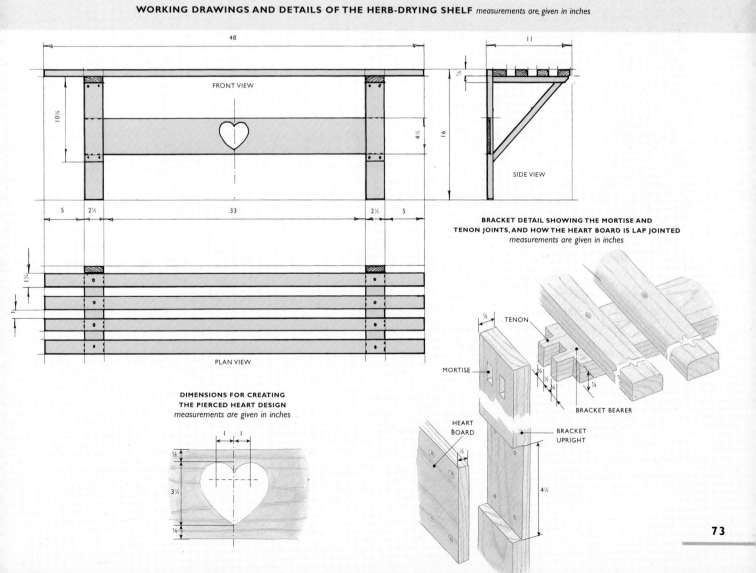

FRONT VIEW

SIDE VIEW

PLAN VIEW

BRACKET DETAIL SHOWING THE MORTISE AND TENON JOINTS, AND HOW THE HEART BOARD IS LAP JOINTED
measurements are given in inches

DIMENSIONS FOR CREATING THE PIERCED HEART DESIGN
measurements are given in inches

TENON

MORTISE

BRACKET BEARER

HEART BOARD

BRACKET UPRIGHT

to set out the shapes that go to make up the joint – the twin tenons and the corresponding mortises (step 3). Aim for tenons at ⅜ in wide, with the spacing at about ½ in.

The procedure for cutting the tenons is… run cuts down to the shoulder line, remove the waste with the backsaw and coping saw (step 4), and pare the waste to the gauged line.

The procedure for cutting the mortises is… set the chisel down with its back to the center, make repeated chops away from center, reverse and rerun the chops at the other side of the center, and scoop out the waste (step 5). Rerun this procedure on both sides of the wood, and then turn the chisel about face and pare the ends to a finish. Finally, trim and ease the joint to a good fit.

Cutting the bracket laps

Take the width and thickness measurements from the heart board, square them around the bracket uprights, and run a gauge line to link the squared lines – the squared lines to establish the shoulders, and the gauged line to fix the depth of the lap.

Run a series of saw cuts across the waste and use the widest possible chisel to pare the resultant ridge down to the base of the lap (step 6). Finally, use a shoulder or small rabbet plane to clean up the shoulders and flatten the base.

Assembly

When you have made all the component parts, it is time to have a dry run put-together. Take the six parts that go to make the two brackets, tap the mortise and tenon joints together (step 7), check the squareness, and screw the brace in position. Set the two brackets 33 in apart, center the

heart board in place in the laps, and run screws through from the back (step 8) – so that the joint is firm, and so that the boards and the screws are all flush. Finally, set the battens across the bracket bearers, check for squareness and spacing, and screw them in place (step 9). If you have got it right, the brackets will finish up being set about 5 in along from the ends of the battens.

Finishing

When you are entirely satisfied with the total fit of the shelf, disassemble the components, cut the ends of the heart board back so that they are

flush with the sides of the bracket uprights, and use the graded sandpapers to rub down all surfaces to a smooth finish. Spend extra time on the end-grain ends – the ends of the battens, and the ends of the bearers that look to the front. Rub the sawn edges of the heart to a slightly rounded finish – so that they feel smooth to the touch. Glue and screw the shelf back together, clean up the dust and give all the surfaces a thin coat of Danish oil. When the oil is dry, rub down the raised grain. Burnish all the surfaces with beeswax, and … the shelf is finished and ready to grace your kitchen or storage room.

DESIGN VARIATIONS

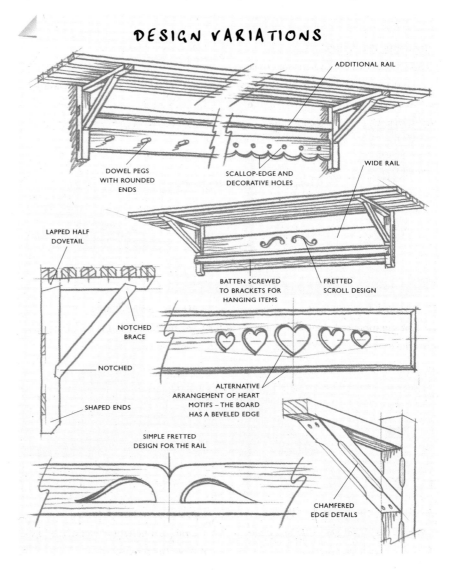

ADDITIONAL RAIL

DOWEL PEGS WITH ROUNDED ENDS

SCALLOP-EDGE AND DECORATIVE HOLES

WIDE RAIL

LAPPED HALF DOVETAIL

BATTEN SCREWED TO BRACKETS FOR HANGING ITEMS

FRETTED SCROLL DESIGN

NOTCHED BRACE

NOTCHED

ALTERNATIVE ARRANGEMENT OF HEART MOTIFS – THE BOARD HAS A BEVELED EDGE

SHAPED ENDS

SIMPLE FRETTED DESIGN FOR THE RAIL

CHAMFERED EDGE DETAILS

MAKING THE HERB-DRYING SHELF

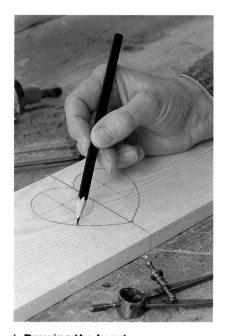

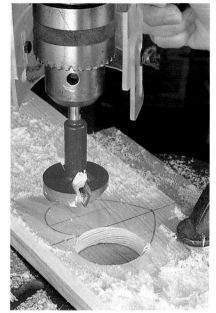

3 Setting out the tenons

Set the gauge to width and mark off the tenons from the shoulder line.

1 Drawing the heart

Use the pencil, rule and dividers to set out the shape of the heart. Note the punched circle centers, and the way the two circles meet on the center line.

2 Piercing the heart

Center the drill bit on the punched center and gently run the hole through. Work at a steady rate to minimize the damage when the drill breaks through.

4 Cutting the tenons

Use a coping saw to clear the waste. Cut to the waste side of the drawn line.

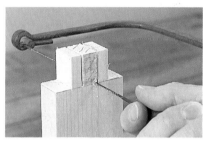

5 Cutting the mortises

Cut the mortise by chiseling out from the center towards the ends.

7 Fixing the brackets

Set the bearer in the vise and push the joint together.

9 Screwing on the battens

Set the battens square and screw them to the bracket bearers.

6 Cutting the bracket joints

Press the chisel down flat and clear the waste with a shearing cut.

8 Fixing the heart board

Drill pilot holes and countersinks, and drive the screws home.

TROUBLESHOOTING

- If you are not keen on mortise and tenon joints, then you could use dowels that run through the uprights and into the ends of the bearers.

- If you like the idea of the pierced heart but don't have a large-size forstner bit, you could cut the heart out with a fretsaw, coping saw, or keyhole saw.

15: DESIGNER BOOKCASE

This impressive bookcase is built in the spirit of the "Mission" style of furniture that was made in America around 1910 by the Roycroft workshops. Founded by Elbert Hubbard, the Mission style is characterized by being massively built and almost totally free from embellishment.

TOOLS AND MATERIALS

- band saw or rip saw, or pre-milled lumber
- crosscut saw
- small backsaw
- coping saw (or bow saw)
- bench, block, and rabbet planes
- square, dividers, rule, and pencil
- single-pin gauge and mortise gauge
- marking knife
- heavy mortise chisel or general bevel of ¾ in, and a wide one of about 1⅛ in
- power sander and graded sandpaper
- clamps
- Danish oil and beeswax polish
- American oak (see cutting list)

CUTTING LIST

part	quantity	L x W x T
oak side boards	2	71 x 11½ x 1¾
fixed shelves	3	17¾ x 11½ x 1¾
removable shelves	4	15⅛ x 11½ x 1¾

(finished sizes, given in inches)

The "Designer" name comes from the fact that Elbert Hubbard punched home his advertising claims that, "Our furniture is individually designed by artists" by having every piece prominently incised with his orb and cross motif – his designer label.

Considering the design

Look at the working drawings and notes. See how this beautifully direct design is made up from the same pretty massive 1¾ in section throughout – for the shelves and the sides. As to whether you need to use such hefty wood, all we can say is that the thick sections are not only good on the eye, but they also help to give the structure its stability. The cleverness of the design idea is that while the top, bottom, and middle shelves are housed and tenoned into the sides to create the basic column structure, the other four shelves can be shifted around to suit your needs.

Preparing the wood•

Take your nine boards – all planed down to a uniform thickness of 1¾ in, all squared true, and with the face sides and edges clearly marked – and check them over for awkwardly placed knots, and for splits that run back into the end grain. One board at a time, measure about ¼ in along from one end, slide the try square up to the mark, and use a knife to square the mark around the wood.

Measure the desired length along from the squared line, repeat the squaring procedure on the other end, and use a saw to cut the wood to length. Finally, secure the workpiece in the vise – with a supporting block and clamp – and use the block plane to bring the end grain to a smooth, square finish.

Laying out the joints

Having worked the two long boards to precisely the same length, set them side by side and use a pencil, rule and square to set out each board with the seven dados or housings that go to make up the design. Use a square to

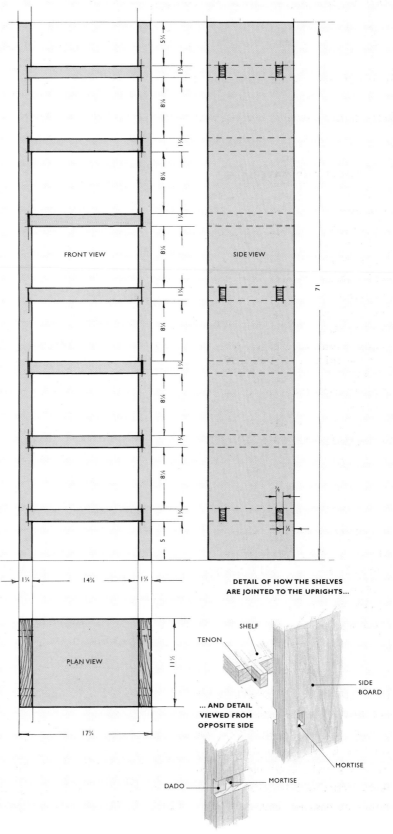

WORKING DRAWINGS AND DETAIL OF THE DESIGNER BOOKCASE
measurements are given in inches

FRONT VIEW

SIDE VIEW

5¼

1¾

8¼

1¾

8¼

1¾

8¼

1¾

8¼

1¾

8¼

1¾

8¼

1¾

5

71

⅞

½

1¾   14⅛   1¾

PLAN VIEW

11½

17¼

DETAIL OF HOW THE SHELVES
ARE JOINTED TO THE UPRIGHTS...

SHELF

TENON

SIDE
BOARD

... AND DETAIL
VIEWED FROM
OPPOSITE SIDE

MORTISE

DADO

MORTISE

run the top, bottom, and middle dados around to what will be the outside face of the board. Flip the two boards over so that they are outside-face uppermost, and set out the precise position of the mortise holes (step 1). Take the three slightly longer shelf boards – the boards to be jointed – and use the pencil, rule and square to lay out the tenons (step 2).

Cutting the dados

First, make absolutely sure that all fourteen dados are precisely set out – in the correct position and at the same width as the shelves. Clamp a guide strip across and against the outside edge of one dado – as marked by the squared line – and use a backsaw to cut the line in to a depth of ½ in. Rerun this procedure on both sides of all fourteen dados.

Use the rabbet plane to lower the waste to the depth of the guide cuts (step 3). Run the plane in from both ends so as to avoid split-out damage. Finally, use a wide chisel to pare down to the drawn line (step 4). The removable shelves should be a sliding fit.

Cutting the mortises

Clamp the workpiece over a well-supported part of the bench – over the top of one of the bench legs – and use the heavy mortise chisel to chop out the mortise. Position the chisel with its back to the center line, run chopped cuts away from the center, increase the depth as the chisel moves to the end, rerun for the other end, and then clean the ends with paring cuts. When you have chopped halfway through the thickness, turn the wood over and chop in from the other side (step 5). Pare the ends of the mortise to a clean finish – so that they run smoothly into the dados.

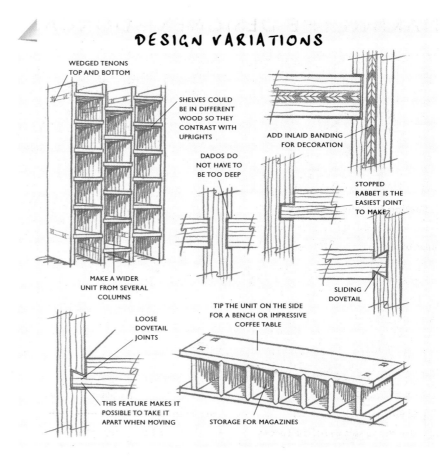

DESIGN VARIATIONS

WEDGED TENONS TOP AND BOTTOM

SHELVES COULD BE IN DIFFERENT WOOD SO THEY CONTRAST WITH UPRIGHTS

ADD INLAID BANDING FOR DECORATION

DADOS DO NOT HAVE TO BE TOO DEEP

STOPPED RABBET IS THE EASIEST JOINT TO MAKE

MAKE A WIDER UNIT FROM SEVERAL COLUMNS

SLIDING DOVETAIL

LOOSE DOVETAIL JOINTS

TIP THE UNIT ON THE SIDE FOR A BENCH OR IMPRESSIVE COFFEE TABLE

THIS FEATURE MAKES IT POSSIBLE TO TAKE IT APART WHEN MOVING

STORAGE FOR MAGAZINES

Cutting the tenons

Having first made sure that your laid-out tenons are perfectly aligned with the cut mortises – you might well need to adjust the marking slightly to fit – set the wood in the vise and start by running cuts down to the shoulder line. Make sure that the cuts are fractionally to the waste side of the drawn line. Use the coping or bow saw to cut the waste from between the tenons, and the backsaw to cut the waste from the shoulders. Use the wide chisel to pare back all the sawn faces to the drawn lines (step 6). Finally – and this is optional – run saw cuts diagonally across the pins, and cut wedges to fit.

Assembly

When you have made all the component parts – two sides and seven shelves – all planed and jointed, set them down on the bench and check them over for fit and possible problems. Set the top, middle, and bottom shelves in place, and gently ease the tenons into their mating mortises, and the shoulders into the dados (step 7). Trim back the ends of the tenons to a clean, flush finish.

Finishing

When you are satisfied with the way the structure comes together, identify the joints with a pencil – so that you know precisely what goes where and how – and then disassemble the shelf unit. Glue and clamp up, drive the wedges home (step 8), and leave overnight. Finally, pare the ends of the wedges flush, clean up the dust, give all the surfaces a thin coat of Danish oil, burnish the whole work with beeswax, and adjust the arrangement of the shelves to suit your needs.

MAKING THE DESIGNER BOOKCASE

Setting out the mortises
Mark out mortises, 1½ in in from the sides of the board, and ⅞ in wide.

2 **Laying out the tenons**
Use the square to set the tenons out on the trued end grain.

3 **Planing the dados**
Tune the rabbet plane so it makes the finest cut and run in from both edges of the board. Repeat this procedure for all fourteen dados.

4 **Paring the dados**
Use the wide chisel to cut the waste down to the gauged line.

5 **Cutting the mortises**
Chop out the mortises with the heavy chisel and the mallet.

6 **Cleaning the tenons**
Pare the shoulders down to the gauged line. Hold the chisel down flat, and run it forward at a slightly angled shearing cut.

7 **Assembling**
Dry-fit the tenons in the mortises and check for a good fit. If it is necessary, use the broad chisel to trim the mortises and the dados.

8 **Wedging the tenons**
Cut wedges to fit, brush glue into the tenon slots, and tap them home.

TROUBLESHOOTING

- While we made all seven shelves — but only used six (see the main picture on page 76) — you could cut costs by only making as many shelves as you need.

- If your mortise and tenon joints are a perfect tight fit, you can opt for leaving out the wedges — as shown in the main picture.

INDEX